STUDY GUIDES
General Editors: John Peck and Martin Coyle

Palgrave Study Guides

A Handbook of Writing for Engineers *Joan van Emden*
Authoring a PhD *Patrick Dunleavy*
Effective Communication for Arts and Humanities Students
   Joan van Emden and Lucinda Becker
Effective Communication for Science and Technology *Joan van Emden*
How to Manage your Arts, Humanities and Social Science Degree
   Lucinda Becker
How to Manage your Science and Technology Degree
   Lucinda Becker and David Price
How to Study Foreign Languages *Marilyn Lewis*
How to Write Better Essays *Bryan Greetham*
Key Concepts in Politics *Andrew Heywood*
Making Sense of Statistics *Michael Wood*
The Mature Student's Guide to Writing *Jean Rose*
The Postgraduate Research Handbook *Gina Wisker*
Professional Writing *Sky Marsen*
Research Using IT *Hilary Coombes*
Skills for Success *Stella Cottrell*
The Student's Guide to Writing *John Peck and Martin Coyle*
The Study Skills Handbook (second edition) *Stella Cottrell*
Study Skills for Speakers of English as a Second Language *Marilyn Lewis and*
   Hayo Reinders
Studying Economics *Brian Atkinson and Susan Johns*
Studying History (second edition) *Jeremy Black and Donald M. MacRaild*
Studying Mathematics and its Applications *Peter Kahn*
Studying Modern Drama (second edition) *Kenneth Pickering*
Studying Psychology *Andrew Stevenson*
Teaching Study Skills and Supporting Learning *Stella Cottrell*

Palgrave Study Guides: Literature

General Editors: John Peck and Martin Coyle

How to Begin Studying English Literature (third edition) *Nicholas Marsh*
How to Study a Jane Austen Novel (second edition) *Vivien Jones*
How to Study Chaucer (second edition) *Rob Pope*
How to Study a Charles Dickens Novel *Keith Selby*
How to Study an E. M. Forster Novel *Nigel Messenger*
How to Study James Joyce *John Blades*
How to Study Linguistics (second edition) *Geoffrey Finch*
How to Study Modern Poetry *Tony Curtis*
How to Study a Novel (second edition) *John Peck*
How to Study a Poet (second edition) *John Peck*
How to Study a Renaissance Play *Chris Coles*
How to Study Romantic Poetry (second edition) *Paul O'Flinn*
How to Study a Shakespeare Play (second edition) *John Peck and Martin Coyle*
How to Study Television *Keith Selby and Ron Cowdery*
Linguistic Terms and Concepts *Geoffrey Finch*
Literary Terms and Criticism (third edition) *John Peck and Martin Coyle*
Practical Criticism *John Peck and Martin Coyle*

The Mature Student's Guide to Writing

Jean Rose

palgrave

First published 2001 by
PALGRAVE
Houndmills, Basingstoke, Hampshire RG21 6XS and
175 Fifth Avenue, New York, N.Y. 10010
Companies and representatives throughout the world

PALGRAVE is the new global academic imprint of
St. Martin's Press LLC Scholarly and Reference Division and
Palgrave Publishers Ltd (formerly Macmillan Press Ltd).

ISBN 0–333–72520–4

This book is printed on paper suitable for recycling and
made from fully managed and sustained forest sources.

A catalogue record for this book is available
from the British Library.

10   9   8   7   6
10 09 08 07 06 05 04 03

Printed in China

Contents

Acknowledgements

The author would like to thank the following:

AQA for permission to reprint a section of the AEB A-level English paper (0623/1) from summer 1997.

Auto Express for permission to quote from 'Mercedes Benz 190' in 'Going Deutsch', published on 5 January 2000.

Curtis Brown on behalf of Barry Norman for permission to quote from the article 'Rebel with a Cause' (*Radio Times*, vol. 304, no. 3959.54) Copyright © Barry Norman.

Mrs Roma Fletcher for permission to quote from her husband Ronald Fletcher's book, *The Family and Marriage in Britain*, published by Pelican in 1966 (first published by Penguin in 1962).

The *Guardian* for permission to quote from the following reports published on 6 November 1999: 'Cyclone's needless deaths' © Suzanne Goldenberg and 'From here ... to down there – runaway vehicle's rampage' © Geoffrey Gibbs.

The Independent Syndication for permission to quote from the following report published on 7 August 1999: 'Football Will be the Death of Scots' by Roger Dobson.

Intermediate Technology Development Group Ltd (ITDG), Bourton Hall, Bourton-on-Dunsmore, Rugby CV23 9QZ, for permission to reprint the article, 'Power to the People' which was used in the AEB examination noted above.

Oxford University Press for permission to quote from *'Master Harold' ... and the Boys* by Athol Fugard © Athol Fugard 1983 in *Selected Plays* (1987).

Professor P. S. Atiyah for permission to quote from his letter 'One law for us ...', published in *The Independent* on 6 February 2000.

Lyn Jenkins for permission to quote from his letter 'Listen to the Farmers', published in *The Independent* on 6 February 2000.

Bob Mann for permission to quote from his article 'Plymouth City Centre', published in *Devon Life* in January 1998.

All the adult students I have taught (without whom this book would not have been written), and especially those who were kind enough to let me use some of their work here. All names have been changed.

Every effort has been made to trace all the copyright-holders, but if any have been inadvertently overlooked the author and publishers will be pleased to make the necessary arrangement at the earliest opportunity.

Who Is this Book For?

This book is for adults. You are likely to be a mature student, but you may be studying anything from design technology to drama or from business studies to social work. If you are having difficulties with your written English, but can't work out what's wrong, this book will prove invaluable. If you missed out at school or have forgotten some of the rules of grammar, you'll find help here. You may have tried looking at books that give grammatical rules but then found that you couldn't relate these to your own situation. This book will take you slowly and gently through the basics of good writing at your own pace. Many of the explanations and examples have been deliberately kept simple in order to make the process as stress-free as possible.

You may have started an Access to Higher Education course. Maybe you are an Open University student or you are studying part-time at a college of higher education. You may be a science student who has always found English baffling. Perhaps you are not a student at all, but just want to brush up your skills. Whatever you are doing, you'll find lots of tips here to help you with writing well and improving your style.

How to Use this Book

There are a number of different ways you can use this book. What you do will depend very much on your own individual circumstances – on how much you remember from school, for instance, or on what particular assignments you have to cope with. You'll probably find that there are some things you just need to brush up on and others that you need to look at more carefully. You are likely to find that you will need to cover one or two issues immediately and some as they arise in relation to your course or other work.

You may have just begun an Access course. Perhaps you have been asked to write a letter for an assignment. You are likely to want to look at chapter 11, in Part Three, so that you can get the main structure right straight away. When your tutor has seen and commented on the letter, you may find that you need some help with understanding how verbs work. That will be the time to turn back to the beginning of Part One and read chapters 1 and 2 on how to use verbs accurately in your sentences.

If you find, for example, that you need to brush up your knowledge of verbs, or are just feeling a bit rusty, you might like to scan the introduction in chapter 1 and then turn straight to the summary at the end of the chapter to see if it makes sense to you. If it rings bells and you feel fairly confident, you could turn back to the activities and try one or two to test yourself. This may be all you need.

If, however, things are not coming back easily, or if an item is quite new to you, you'll probably want to work through the whole chapter. It would be a good idea to take one section at a time when you have a spare 20 minutes or so, rather than trying to do too much at once. This way, you won't overload yourself with new information.

On the other hand, you may already be in higher education but have never quite got to grips with verbs and sentence structure. In that case, after brushing up on chapters 1 and 2, you'll probably want to read chapter 8 on clauses.

You can also use the book as a quick reference tool. Perhaps you want to know what an adjective is, or how to use a semicolon. Just turn to the index and this will refer you to the page you need.

Always give new information time to sink in. Learning to improve your writing is not like learning a set of dates. You will need to practise each skill that is new to you. So don't be alarmed if you continue to make mistakes for a little while. Expect to improve gradually. When your tutor marks an error in your writing, go back to the rules so that you understand *exactly* what went wrong. It is through fully understanding our errors that we are able to make most progress.

Part One is about the basics of clear and grammatically correct sentences. If you need help with specific issues, you'll find it here.

Each chapter begins with a brief introduction. This is followed by explanations (with rules) and activities for practice. At the end of the chapter, you'll find a summary of the main points you need to remember. These chapters are designed to give you the skills for writing clear sentences. One of the reasons that you may be having difficulties with your writing is that you are just not aware of all the rules. Part I will help you here.

Part Two looks in detail at essay-writing. It will take you through the whole process. There is a separate chapter on note-taking and referencing, and another on writing more complex sentences. If you are new to studying, work through chapter 6 and leave the other two chapters in Part Two until you feel that you need them. The introductions and summaries will help you to remember key points.

Part Three covers particular writing tasks you are likely to be doing and gives some examples of how students have approached these. The first chapter – chapter 9 – forms a basis for each of the others. It contains important material on how to adjust your writing for different types of assignment. Again, introductions and chapter summaries will help to make things clear.

If You Think You May Be Dyslexic . . .

There are many forms of dyslexia. As well as causing problems with writing, these can affect various other activities, particularly your ability to organize your work. It's possible, of course, that you are not dyslexic at all. Sometimes, well-meaning friends can suggest that a person is dyslexic just because his or her spelling is not good. You will need to be tested in order to be quite sure what the problem is.

Most colleges and universities now provide tests for dyslexia and are keen to do all they can to help. Even students in evening classes can apply for the test if they are studying for an exam. Sometimes, notes and handouts can be provided in a special format for those who are dyslexic, and sometimes a laptop computer can be obtained for your personal use. Extra time can be allowed in examinations, and sometimes a student can be allocated someone to help take notes in class sessions. All this takes time to organize, so it's important to apply for testing as early as possible in the academic year. If you leave this too late, help may not be available, or you may have fallen so far behind that it's difficult to catch up.

If it turns out that you are dyslexic, you will need to ask your college how you can make use of this book. It is unlikely that you will be able to work through it in the same way as a student who is not dyslexic. So make sure that you take advice. This book does *not* contain any specific help with dyslexia.

Part One
The Nuts and Bolts of Good Writing

1 Verbs

INTRODUCTION

This chapter will explain verbs in detail and how they work. If you are completely new to verbs, you will need to read the whole chapter, but if you know something about them already, you'll probably find that you want to skip bits of it.

If you are having trouble writing grammatical sentences, it's ten to one that the key to the problem is your use of verbs. Once you understand what a verb is, you'll be able to make good use of chapter 2. You will not need to learn what follows by heart. For example, unless you are studying languages, you certainly won't need to be able to spot the **tense** of a verb (see below). However, once you have an *understanding* of how verbs work, you will be able to write well-formed sentences without too much trouble.

You may have terrible memories of having been unable to learn verbs at school, or you may never have been taught anything about them at all, but fear not. Like all other aspects of written English, there's no mystique to verbs and you will soon understand how they work. In any case, we all use them expertly when we speak – without having to think at all. You might like to think of a verb as being the spark that gets the engine going. A verb is the central key to every well-written sentence.

Think, for a moment, of a dictionary that contains all the words in the English language. Each one of these words can do a particular job in a sentence. There are eight basic jobs, and these are done by eight different **parts of speech**: nouns, verbs, adjectives, adverbs, pronouns, conjunctions, prepositions and interjections. If you are dead keen, you can find out about all eight, but you'll probably never need more than the first five, and if you manage just the first two, your control of your writing will improve enormously. The most important are verbs.

▶ Doing words

If your school used to teach verbs, you may remember that verbs are often called 'doing' words. Most verbs tell us something about some kind of *action*. Here are some examples:

run	drink
swim	breathe
blink	laugh
walk	drive
eat	talk

It's easy to imagine somebody (or perhaps some animal) doing most of those things, isn't it? They are all actions. Let's put some of them into sentences. We may have to alter some of them very slightly to make them sound right:

Jenny **runs** for her school in league fixtures.
We usually **blink** several times a minute.
Both my children **walk** to school.
Most of the time, we **breathe** very quietly.
Carl **works** on the shop floor.
Many people **drive** to work.
Politicians **talk** a lot.

There are other things we do that may not show up quite so clearly, but which still count as actions. Here are some examples of these:

love	remember
hate	plan
wonder	want
calculate	think

And here are some of them in sentences:

Jamie **loves** curry.
Cindy **hates** the dentist.
I **wonder** how old Jack is?
My grandfather **remembers** the First World War.

I **want** lots of money.
Ben **likes** jazz and **loves** the blues.

You have probably noticed that there are actually *two* verbs in the last sentence. If we wanted, we could put more in:

Ben **likes** jazz, **loves** the blues, **buys** CDs, and **goes** to concerts every month.

ACTIVITY 1

See if you can pick out the verbs in the following sentences and write them down. There is just one in each. Remember that you are looking for words which tell you what somebody or something *does*.

1 I wash the car on Saturdays.
2 Horoscopes foretell the future.
3 The farmers long for rain.
4 Before winter, many birds migrate to warmer lands.
5 Jeanne sends faxes to America.
6 We all desire happiness.

Feedback

I expect you got most of those right, but don't worry if you didn't. Making mistakes is all part of the learning process. You might like to try another exercise.

ACTIVITY 2

As in Activity 1, write down the verb from each sentence:

1 My son daydreams in his French lessons.
2 Enrico works seven days a week.
3 Before breakfast, Jim delivers papers.
4 Sam and Tom like movies.
5 Many people pray for peace.
6 Australia exports wine.

▶ Time

When we speak, we all use verbs expertly to show *when* something happens. Let's look at my very first example and imagine that Jenny's mother is speaking to a friend:

> "Jenny **runs** for her school in league fixtures."

Her mother means that whenever there's a league race, Jenny is in it. This is the current state of affairs – it tells us about what is happening in the **present**.

Let's suppose that Jenny has now grown up, and that her mother is recalling her schooldays in a letter to a friend. She might say:

> Jenny **ran** for her school in league fixtures.

She's now talking about what Jenny did in the **past**. While she is recalling what used to happen, Jenny's mother might want to talk about different times in the past. In that letter, she might go on to say:

> By the time she **was** fifteen, Jenny **had run** in ten league fixtures.

The word *had* used with a verb is very useful for showing that something happened further back in the past than another period we are referring to.

Let's suppose that Jenny has only just been picked to run for the school, and that her mother is explaining what this means in a letter to Jenny's grandmother:

> Jenny **will run** for the school in league matches.

Now Jenny's mother is talking about the future.

Sometimes, a verb has more than one part to it. Notice that that is the case here: the parts are *will* and *run*.

The **verbs** in those four sentences are written to show whether something happens in the **present** (*runs*), the **past** (*ran* and *had run*), or the **future** (*will run*). There's a word for this: **tense**. We can say that those four sentences are written in different **tenses**: the **present tense**, the **past tense**, the **past perfect tense**, and the **future tense**.

The **past perfect tense** is the one that uses the word *had*.

We can look at another sentence from that first batch:

Both my children **walk** to school.

This is obviously a parent writing about what is going on now. It is written in the **present tense**.

If we imagine that the family has recently moved further away from the school and now owns a car, this parent might write:

Until very recently, both my children **walked** to school.

You can see that the parent is now looking at what used to happen in the **past**, so is writing in the **past tense**.

But maybe things have worked out differently. Perhaps the family owned a car, but has had to sell it. The parent might now write:

From now on, both my children **will walk** to school.

This tells us about what will happen in the future, so we can say it is written in the **future tense**. Here we've got another verb with two parts: *will* and *walk*.

ACTIVITY 3

Look at the following sentences, and write down **past**, **past perfect**, **present** or **future** for each one:

1 Margaret Thatcher led Britain's Conservative party for many years.
2 America's President lives at the White House.
3 Napoleon won many battles.
4 Denise will sit her final exams in June.
5 I go to my guitar lesson once a week.
6 All the members of the club had been to the previous meeting.
7 At 10 p.m., the supermarket will close.
8 Some animals hibernate in winter.
9 Mark will get redundancy pay from his employer.
10 Sophie had never played better than on Saturday.

Continuous action (sometimes called **progressive**)
There's one final thing I want to explain here about **tenses**. We can show (and remember that we all do these things so easily when we speak) whether or not an action goes on happening in either the past, present or future. This is called **continuous** action:

Last week, Martin **was thinking** about a holiday.	**past continuous**
John **is thinking** about a holiday.	**present continuous**
Soon, Cherie **will be thinking** about a holiday.	**future continuous**

In each sentence, the person doing the thinking is spending quite a bit of time at it – the action is *continuing* over a period. Notice that, in each case, the final part of the verb ends in *ing*. You can see from the third sentence that a verb can have three parts. (Later on, we'll find some with four.)

Here's a little table that you can use as a checklist:

I will wash the car next Saturday morning.	**future**
I will be washing the car after breakfast.	**future continuous**
I wash the car every week.	**present**
I am washing the car now.	**present continuous**
I washed the car last week.	**past**
I was washing the car with a new shampoo.	**past continuous**
I had washed the car before lunch.	**past perfect**
I had been washing the car all morning.	**past perfect continuous**

ACTIVITY 4

Write down the tense for each verb in the following sentences:

1 I want a drink.
2 Maud broke her false teeth.
3 Mark will laugh at the photo.
4 After the exams, the students will be celebrating.
5 Marie is eating her breakfast.
6 Stan had considered the problem.
7 Angélique will be cooking this evening.

8 We went to Disneyland last year.
9 I had been coughing all morning.
10 The children were riding their bikes round the playground.

▶ The verb *to be*

The verb *to be* has nothing at all to do with 'doing'. You might have heard of this verb because it's used in a very famous speech from William Shakespeare's *Hamlet:*

To be or not to be. That is the question ...

In the play, Hamlet's father, the old king, has been murdered, and his ghost appears to Hamlet asking him to take revenge and kill the murderer. The old king has actually been murdered by his brother, who has seized the throne and married the old king's wife.

Killing does not come easily to Hamlet, who is a scholar and not a fighter, and he spends a great deal of the play just trying to decide what to do. He even considers the possibility of suicide, and when he says, "To be or not to be" he is thinking about life and death – existence or non-existence.

The verb *to be* may look rather insignificant, but it does some very important work. If you are interested in New Age therapies and ideas, you may have heard of the idea of just 'being'. Some people, exhausted with what they see as the 'rat race' of modern life, have decided that they no longer want to rush around 'doing' things but that they prefer just 'being'.

The verb *to be* is the one we use when we want to describe things. It probably gets more use than any other verb.

Describing people, animals and things

The following words are all parts of the verb *to be*: **is, am, are, was, were**, and **will be**. We use one or the other of them whenever we describe anything, or when we give a brief explanation about it. Here they are in some sentences:

I **am** a woman.
You **are** wonderful.
Alan **is** Australian.

You **were** the winner.
Hamlet **was** depressed.
The footballers **were** muddy after the match.

The train **will be** late.
The carnival **will be** exciting.
The runners **will be** tired.

You may have noticed that each of those three groups of sentences is written in a different tense – present, past and future.

The verb to be as an auxiliary (i.e. a helping) verb
In the three sentences showing continuous action on page 8, I used the words *was*, *is* and *will be* to help to put the verb *to think* into different continuous tenses. This means that I was using parts of the verb *to be* together with an action verb. You will find that this happens a lot. The verb *to be* is a very useful one.

There are also some other verbs that are known as **auxiliaries**, but unless you are studying English grammar at university, you are unlikely to need to know much about them. It's worth looking out, however, for the verb **have** which, like items from the verb *to be*, is used quite often. For example:

1 I **have been studying** for two hours.
2 By next month, I **will have been studying** for two years.

In the first sentence here, you can see that the verb has three parts, and in the second, four.

The verb *to have* is another one which, like the verb *to be*, is very versatile. You could say that it wears a number of different hats. The next section will explain another of its jobs.

▶ **Having**

Those in the know will tell you that verbs are about three things – doing, being and having. We've looked at the first two of these, so all we have left now is a *very* small group of words that tell us about owning things: *to have*, *to own*, *to possess*, *to inherit* and *to get*. Here are some examples of them in use:

Joe **has** a cupboard full of cricket gear.
Chris **owns** a pub.
Aladdin **possessed** a magic lamp.
Linda **will inherit** her mother's house.
Lizzie **got** a bargain in the sales.

ACTIVITY 5

Underline the verbs in the following sentences and note down whether each is a 'doing', 'being' or 'having' verb. There is only one verb in each sentence, but it may have more than one part.

1 Mary ate a pomegranate.
2 Max has six fossils.
3 We will be crossing the border at six tonight.
4 The earth goes round the sun.
5 The lions were very hungry.
6 The view from the mountain is beautiful.
7 The dog had fleas.
8 Terry will have £300 by next month.
9 The flies were buzzing round the meat.
10 The calculation will be difficult.

If you have been working on these verbs for a while, I suggest you have a break before starting on the next section on **actives** and **passives**. It's quite a short section, but it's a little bit tricky and needs careful thought.

▶ Actives and passives

In a simple sentence, the person at the beginning can usually be seen to be *doing* the verb, so to speak. We call this type of verb **active**. But sometimes, the verb is being done *to* him or her. This is a **passive** verb. The difference between **active** and **passive** verbs shows up in the following two sentences:

I was bitten by the dog.	**passive**
I bit the dog.	**active**

In the first sentence, the biting was done *to* me. In the second, I did it. In both sentences, the focus is on *I*. If I really had been bitten by a dog (as in the first sentence) I'd be likely to say:

The dog bit me.

You can see that the focus is now on what the *dog* did. It has become the most important item in the sentence. Now that I've changed the verb from passive to active, the sentence has also become much more lively. These days, we don't use the passive much because it often seems rather cold and dead.

Have a look at the next two sentences:

I was trodden on by the baby.
I trod on the baby.

Nowadays, instead of the first of these sentences, we'd be much more likely to say:

The baby trod on me.

This is much more simple and lively. It's more informal, too.

Below are some active and passive verbs. Look carefully at these as they will help you to be clear on the differences.

ACTIVE	PASSIVE
Present	
Maisie **is** watching the parrot.	The parrot **is being watched** by Maisie.
Hazel **likes** everyone.	Everyone **is liked** by Hazel.
Past	
I **bit** the dog.	The dog **was bitten** by me.
Sue **phoned** the TV company.	The TV company **was phoned** by Sue.
Future	
Tim **will give** a vote of thanks.	A vote of thanks **will be given** by Tim.
The President of the United States **will meet** the Russian envoy.	The Russian envoy **will be met** by the President of the United States.

Note that with passives, the person *preceding* the verb (who you'd normally expect to be 'doing' it) is having it done *to* him or her.

Don't worry about how to write passives – you'll do it automatically. I'm showing you here how to *spot* them. Unless you are an English student, the only time you are likely to need to know much about them is if a tutor comments that you are using too many of them. A piece of writing filled with passives can sound rather lifeless. That said, you will find that you will need to use them in report-writing. (See chapter 13.)

You will find that the passive is used for the following jobs:

- focusing on the *receiver* of an action
- writing up *reports* and scientific *experiments*
- showing that the *doer* of the action is *unknown*.

Here's an example of that last item:

The baby was abandoned in the church.

Because we don't know who did the abandoning, the only way we could make that sentence active would be to say:

Someone abandoned the baby in the church.

If you find all this tricky to follow, come back to it after you have worked through the section on **subjects** and **objects** in chapter 2.

ACTIVITY 6

Mark each of the following sentences A or P for active or passive:

1 The priest tripped over the bridesmaid's foot.
2 Food was provided by the bride's sister and her husband.
3 The couple's friends were greeted by the bride's parents.
4 The bride wore a beautiful dress.
5 All the speeches were brief.
6 The bride was given a kiss by the groom.
7 The little bridesmaid was looked after by her mother.
8 The wedding guests were served by catering students.
9 A journalist reported on the wedding in the local paper.
10 The day will be remembered for a long time.

▶ Conjugating (i.e. setting out) verbs

Setting out a verb is a bit of a bother, and you won't ever be asked to do it (unless you are a student of languages), but it can be very useful just to see how it's done. Once you've understood the pattern, you will find that it works for all verbs. It shows how a verb is used for different people.

Remember, you almost certainly do the whole thing accurately when you speak, so all I'm doing here is to show you in diagram form what you actually say. I'll use the verb *to talk*:

The verb *to talk*

Singular			Plural	
		Present		
I	talk		we	talk
you	talk		you	talk
he/she/it	talks		they	talk
		Past		
I	talked		we	talked
you	talked		you	talked
he/she/it	talked		they	talked
		Past perfect		
I	had talked		we	had talked
you	had talked		you	had talked
he/she/it	had talked		they	had talked
		Future		
I	will talk		we	will talk
you	will talk		you	will talk
he/she/it	will talk		they	will talk

The continuous tenses are also very simple:

		Present continuous		
I	am talking		we	are talking
you	are talking		you	are talking
he/she/it	is talking		they	are talking

Past continuous

I	was talking	we	were talking
you	were talking	you	were talking
he/she/it	was talking	they	were talking

Past perfect continuous

I	had been talking	we	had been talking
you	had been talking	you	had been talking
he/she/it	had been talking	they	had been talking

Future continuous

I	will be talking	we	will be talking
you	will be talking	you	will be talking
he/she/it	will be talking	they	will be talking

The verb *to talk* is known as a **regular verb**. Basically, this means that we add *s* for the third-person singular in the present, and *ed* for the past tense. Some verbs are **irregular**, and that can make things a bit difficult for those whose first language is not English.

The verb *to be* is an irregular verb. It is less simple and straightforward than the verb *to run*. This is how it looks when it is set out:

The verb *to be*

Present

I	am	we	are
you	are	you	are
he/she/it	is	they	are

Past

I	was	we	were
you	were	you	were
he/she/it	was	they	were

Past perfect

I	had been	we	had been
you	had been	you	had been
he/she/it	had been	they	had been

Future

I	will be	we	will be
you	will be	you	will be
he/she/it	will be	they	will be

If you are going to study linguistics, you are likely to need to learn a lot more about the finer points of verbs, but the rest of us can get away with knowing just the basics.

So now you have a good idea of what verbs are, you'll find that you can easily work through the chapter on sentences.

SUMMARY

- Verbs tell us about: doing
  being
  having.
- The majority are *action* words – i.e. doing.
- The verb *to be* helps us to *describe* people and things – e.g. *is, are, were.*
- We show *when* something happens through using different *tenses*.
- Many verbs have more than one part.
- *Active* verbs are more lively than *passive* ones.

2 Sentences

INTRODUCTION

If you have read the chapter on verbs, you're now well prepared to check out the rules for writing good sentences. Everybody knows roughly what a sentence is, and this works fine when we leave notes around for people we live or work with or write simple letters to friends. It's when we start to write about complex topics or try to construct tricky business letters that difficulties can arise.

This chapter will cover the basic rules for writing grammatical sentences, as well as one of the most common errors that people make, and a full explanation of grammatical **subjects** and **objects**. Everyone needs to understand the basic rules and be aware of problem areas. A little knowledge of subjects and objects will further enhance your ability to write well. If you are studying English as one of your main subjects, it will be vital for you to understand subjects and objects. If you are not studying English as a main subject, however, you can afford to ignore section II of this chapter.

I THE BASICS

It's not likely to be news to you that a sentence needs to start with a capital letter and end with a full stop. Beyond this, there are three rules for writing good sentences.

A sentence must:

- make sense by itself
- contain a subject
- contain a working verb.

▶ Making sense

When you read the chapter on punctuation, you'll see that the reason we use full stops is to help make our meaning clear. Meaning is crucial for whoever reads what we write. Look at this sentence:

With all his football kit.

I'm sure you can see that there's a problem here. This 'sentence' doesn't make sense, does it? I'd better improve it:

John went to school with all his football kit.

Now you know what I mean. A sentence should always tells us something clearly. It makes some kind of *statement*. In this case, I've communicated information about John going to school with his kit. You may want to know who John is, or the name of the school, and whether John was just practising or was playing in a match, but you now have a basic idea of what was going on.

A good test of whether a sentence works is to check whether someone reading it would be able to ask a sensible question about it, or whether the likely response to it would be a very puzzled "Eh?" My first attempt was only half a sentence, and you probably found it rather confusing. The words I used could have referred to any number of different people or places. They just seem to hang in the air, and it's hard to know what to make of them.

Look at the following extract from Susan's essay on education. She has made a very common error. Most of her sentences are well formed, but while concentrating on explaining what she means, she suddenly forgets the rules:

A majority of children and teenagers benefit greatly from the structure and compulsory nature of school attendance. For many from a background of poverty, school can mean a haven. A warm and stimulating place.

Susan's final sentence doesn't make sense by itself. It is actually part of her explanation in the previous sentence. This piece of writing would have been a lot better if Susan had used a comma after *haven* instead of a full stop.

If a tutor has written 'not a sentence' in the margin of your work, the problem may be that you have not been aware of this first crucial rule. You may have been writing down things as you would have said them. When we speak, we frequently break the rules of written grammar, and we still manage to make ourselves understood. This is because we also use facial expressions, gesture, and tone of voice to get our meaning across.

It's worth looking closely at the kind of thing that happens when we speak. In the following snatch of conversation, look carefully at what Sam's mother says:

"Where are my pyjamas, Mum?" asked Sam.
"On the floor!" replied his mother crossly. "Where you left them."

Sam's mother has spoken two 'sentences', but neither of them makes sense by itself. It's OK for her to say,

"On the floor!"

because Sam knows (a) exactly what is on the floor, and (b) which floor she's referring to. He knows from the tone of her voice that she's cross, and he'll hear the sarcasm in

"Where you left them."

His mother will probably put a heavy stress on the word *left*. She'll probably also use facial expressions and body language to get her meaning across. She may scowl at Sam, toss her head, shrug her shoulders, or turn her back on him. Alternatively, she might try to look unconcerned and just brush him aside to show him she isn't interested in silly questions.

Not only does his mother give lots of extra clues to her meaning, but both Sam and his mother know a good deal about those pyjamas. So when they speak to each other, they can use a kind of shorthand. When we are writing, our sentences must make complete sense by themselves, because whoever reads them cannot hear us or pick up clues from our expressions or body language.

If I were writing a story about Sam and his mother, I would have to explain things very carefully if I were not going to use conversation. I might do it like this:

When Sam pestered his mother to find his pyjamas, she brushed him aside crossly, telling him to go and look for them on his bedroom floor where he had thrown them that morning.

You can see that I've had to give more information to make things quite clear.

ACTIVITY 1

Have a look at the following and see if you can work out which are real sentences – that is, sentences that make clear sense by themselves:

1 about half-past nine
2 you don't often see kangaroos in Britain
3 I want a Coke
4 all by himself
5 whether you like it or not
6 wearing light blue trousers
7 I'm hot

▶ The subject in a sentence

You are probably used to using the word *subject* to mean either *area of study* or *topic*. So if I ask you what subjects you are studying, the answer is likely to be "English and history", or "science and maths", and so on. Or if I ask what was the subject of the lecture you went to yesterday, the answer might be "the poetry of John Keats", or "the French Revolution", or "recycling waste materials".

The word *subject* used in relation to grammar has a rather different meaning. It is closely linked to verbs. You'll remember from chapter 1 that verbs are about doing, being or having.

A sentence always tells us about somebody or something. Look at the following sentences:

Roy ate cheese sandwiches for his lunch.
Sarah sold her car last week.

Each of these sentences gives us information about a particular person. We know what Roy ate, and what Sarah did with her car. Roy is the **subject** of the verb *ate* and Sarah is the **subject** of the verb *sold*.

This rule functions in exactly the same way with animals, birds, insects and things, too:

Polar bears live in the Arctic.
Spiders have eight legs.
The church stands beside the river.
Water freezes at 0° centigrade.

Think back for a moment to the three types of verbs in chapter 1: doing, being and having. Then consider the following statement carefully:

The subject of a verb is the person or thing that is doing the doing, being or having.

In the sentence about polar bears, the verb is *live*. So we can ask ourselves who or what is doing the living. The answer is polar bears. So the subject of the verb *live* is *polar bears*. In the second sentence, we can ask who or what is doing the having, and the answer is spiders. So we now know that the subject of the verb *have* in that particular sentence is spiders.

Remember that the word *subject* here means a *subject for the verb*. Any sentence will have a topic. It can't help being *about something*. But it must also have a grammatical subject for its verb. If we wanted to be specific, we could say that the *topics* of those four sentences above are:

the habits of polar bears
the physiology of spiders
the position of the church
the properties of water

Let's look at some sentences in which the verb is concerned with **being**:

I **am** hot.
Arnold **is** eighty years old.
The river **was** dark and sluggish.
The actors **were** on the stage.

I expect you realized that the grammatical subjects for these sentences are *I*, *Arnold*, *The river*, and *The actors*.

► Working verbs

The third crucial thing for a sentence is that it must contain a **working verb**. By *working verb*, I mean one that is actually doing a job. The good news is that you already know all about this if you've read through the sections on doing, being and having in chapter 1. The verbs that are set out at the end of chapter 1 are shown as we use them to do a wide variety of different jobs. Each is headed by its name: *to talk* and *to be*. The name of a verb is known by the term **infinitive**. So *to talk* and *to be* are both infinitives. They are not doing any specific work, but are just hanging around doing nothing, so to speak.

An infinitive on its own in a sentence won't be enough and it's easy to see why if you look at the following poorly constructed sentence:

I to walk by the sea.

This makes no sense. But if I add a working verb it will be fine:

I like to walk by the sea.

As you can see, it's OK to have an infinitive in a sentence as long as there's a working verb there as well.

By the way, be careful not to confuse the two functions of the word *to*:

I went to Paris.

I like to swim.

In the first sentence, the word *to* introduces a place; in the second, it's part of an infinitive – *to swim*.

ACTIVITY 2

In the following sentences, underline each working verb and then put a ring around the subject of that verb.

1 Jimi Hendrix died young.
2 Beatlemania swept Britain in the 1960s.
3 Fraser plays guitar in a folk band after work.

4 Punk Rock lasted only a short time.
5 Many young girls have wanted to follow in the footsteps of the Spice Girls.
6 Salsa is becoming a highly popular dance.

The lack of a working verb is the cause of by far the greatest proportion of ungrammatical sentences that are written. The really annoying thing is that if you are leaving out verbs, you are probably doing it only occasionally, and so it's often hard to spot just the one or two instances in a piece of work where you've made the error.

I'd like you to look at the following sentence from an essay by Susan, a student on an Access to Higher Education course. The title of the essay was 'Discuss the proposition that education is wasted on the young':

Pressures from their peer group, like keeping up with the latest fad, fashion, and pop sensations.

As it stands, this is confusing. With a small addition, however, it can easily be made to make much better sense:

Young people often encounter pressures from their peer group, like keeping up with the latest fad, fashion, and pop sensations.

Now the sentence has a subject – *Young people*, and a working verb – *encounter*.

This kind of error is very common. If I now show you Susan's previous sentences, you can see how the problem occurred:

In secondary school, mainly, young people come into contact with all sorts of influences as a whole new social scene emerges. These include drink and drugs which, previously, young people would have been sheltered from at primary school. Pressures from their peer group, like keeping up with the latest fad, fashion, and pop sensations.

What happened was that Susan started writing as if she were speaking. She added in another idea without considering how to construct the sentence.

▶ **The infuriating *ing* problem**

The good news is that just as the greatest proportion of errors are caused by the lack of a working verb, the greatest proportion of working-verb difficulties are the result of one specific type of problem. This means that once you are aware of this particular issue, you can quickly learn to look out for it. I call it the *ing* problem.

At the beginning of this chapter, I demonstrated some of the differences between spoken and written speech. What I call the *ing* problem generally occurs when someone is struggling to get a complex idea on paper and lapses momentarily into speech patterns. Here's a simple example:

> Ken had been at the football ground all afternoon. Watching the match.

If I were to read this aloud to a class of students, they would have absolutely no difficulty understanding me. But if you look carefully, you will see that, although the first sentence is fine, the second one has several problems. To start with, it doesn't make sense. It also lacks both a subject and a fully working verb. If you look back at the table of continuous verbs in chapter 1, you'll see that these all have more than one part.

There are two ways we could sort out the example above:

1 Instead of putting a full stop after *afternoon*, we could use a comma. Then the statement about the match becomes a small piece of information added to the first sentence:

> Ken had been at the football ground all afternoon, watching the match.

Now we've got just *one* sentence. The working verb is *had been*, and the subject of that verb is *Ken*.

In this particular sentence, we could omit the comma altogether:

> Ken had been at the football ground all afternoon watching the match.

2 We could make sure that the second sentence has a subject and that the *ing* verb has *at least two parts* to it:

Ken had been at the football ground all afternoon. He **had been watching** the match.

The second sentence now has both a subject (someone doing the *watching* – *He*) and a fully working verb.

All *ing* verbs have at least two parts. Our example above has three – *had been watching* and you'll come across instances where there are four. As long as you remember that any *ing* (continuous) verb at the start of a sentence must have *at least two parts*, you won't go far wrong. This is because, once you've alerted yourself to the problem, your knowledge of the language will automatically supply you with what you need. I promise.

The classic place for the *ing* problem to occur is, as in my example, just after a full stop. Here it is in a more complex piece of writing by Mark, a student on a Science Access course. This is from an article he wrote on sustainable rural development:

> *Even human waste could either be composted or put through a water reed bed purification system. Thus alleviating the need to be connected to the present archaic disposal system in place today.*

The best way of sorting this one out would almost certainly be to change that full stop after *system* to a comma. Otherwise, I think Mark would have to change the wording slightly. He could have begun the second sentence like this:

This type of process would alleviate the need ...

The *ing* problem also occurred in Sandra's opening to her essay on *Hamlet*:

> *Shakespeare ensures that nothing can be taken at face value in the play Hamlet by showing us many different sides to the characters. One side often contradicting another.*

Again, I think the easiest way to sort this one out is to use a comma. With a comma after *characters*, that ungrammatical final sentence would become part of the main sentence, and so the lack of a working verb in those final words is no longer a problem.

If she had wanted to keep that final statement in a separate sentence so that it stands out more, Sandra could have done it in various ways:

(i) One side often contradicts another.

Here, I've used the present simple tense of the verb *to contradict*.

(ii) We often see one side contradicting another.

Now I've added the working verb – *see* – with the subject *we*, so the fact that *contradicting* has only one part does not matter.

(iii) One side is often contradicting another.

Here I've used the present continuous tense, so the verb now has two parts – *is ... contradicting*. The fact that they are separated by another word (*often*) is not a problem.

ACTIVITY 3

Have a go at sorting out the following simple sentences. See if you can do each of them two ways: once as one sentence and once as two. When using one sentence, you may not always want to include a comma. Try to notice whether or not the sense runs straight on. You will probably find only one way of writing number 6.

1 Lucy ran home. Crying all the way.
2 Ken's dog had been annoying the neighbours. Barking all morning.
3 Brad ran down the road with the cheque. Laughing all the way to the bank.
4 The children came home covered in mud. Looking absolutely filthy.
5 English grammar can be difficult. Causing all sorts of problems.
6 I couldn't think how to get the cork out of the bottle. Trying everything I knew.
7 The wolf set off through the forest. Looking for the cottage belonging to Little Red Riding Hood's grandmother.

ACTIVITY 4

Now see if you can sort out these longer sentences. Do each *one* way only.

1 Nursery schools are places where children learn some of the basic skills they will need for primary school. Recognizing their names, making simple models, and getting along with others.

2 My local school has started a monthly newsletter. Believing this will help make local people more aware of all the activities available for children and parents.

3 This essay will look at both sides of the argument in order to show the complexity of the issues involved. Crucial issues affecting every aspect of our lives.

Breaking the rules

There are certain times when rules can be broken. When we write conversation (see chapters 5 and 10), there are likely to be lots of sentences without verbs. You will also find what might appear to be ungrammatical sentences in novels and in journalistic writing. This could be because the material is badly produced, but it is more likely to result from the writer having taken a conscious decision to write in a particular way in order to create a particular effect. Chatty writing sometimes omits verbs; and sometimes omission is used for impact.

It's a good idea, however, to leave this kind of thing to the experts until you are really familiar with writing correctly. It's OK to break the rules once you know what you're doing and why. While you are a student, it's best to play safe. Unless you are on a creative writing course, your tutors are not likely to be very happy to see sentences that lack either verbs or subjects.

A note for people who like to use the correct terminology

The formal name for my term *working verb* is **finite verb**. The word *finite* means *having boundaries*. This is opposite to *the infinitive*, which is open-ended. If you think back to Hamlet's speech that I mentioned in chapter 1 – 'To be or not to be' – you can see that he's thinking about existence and non-existence (in his case, suicide) in a very detached way. He's not making any clear statement about what he'll actually do. For that he would need a working verb.

I also made up the term *ing word* because it is an easy way of referring to those parts of verbs ending in *ing* that can cause difficulties when writing sentences. My term also demonstrates exactly what it is referring to. The correct term is **present participle**. You will find a present participle in any example of a present continuous verb – for example, *barking* in the following sentence:

> The dog **is barking.**

The present participle here – *barking* – is from the verb *to bark*. The *ing* form also appears in the **past continuous** tense. You can tell the tense of a continuous verb from the bits that precede the *ing* word. The present continuous tense uses *is* and are; the past continuous uses *was* and *were*; the future continuous uses *will be*.

The same type of problem as the *ing* problem can occur with a **past participle**, but this happens far less often. A past participle very often ends in *ed*. The past participle of the verb *to bark* is *barked*.

If you are happy with this formal terminology, you will no doubt use it to refer to issues discussed in this chapter. If, like many people, you find jargon a bit intimidating, stick to thinking of *ing* words and *working verbs*.

II MORE ON SUBJECTS AND A LITTLE ON OBJECTS

I explained above that:

> The subject of a verb is the person or thing that is doing the doing, being or having.

The following simple sentences will remind you. I've put the subjects in bold type and the verbs in italics:

John *is squeezing* his spots.	doing
The doctor *was* helpful.	being
The Chemist *has* cream for acne.	having

This is all fairly straightforward. There are, of course (surprise, surprise), a few variations from this that can make it a little more difficult to spot the subject in a sentence. Remember, I'm not talking here about the *topic* of the sentence, but about the subject of the verb.

▶ Longer sentences

You have now seen that every verb has a subject. So in any sentence that contains more than one verb, there will be more than one grammatical subject. For example,

> **The kitchen** *looks* awful since **the dog** *chewed* the curtains and **the baby** *spilt* blackcurrant juice down the wall.

Here there are three verbs so there must be three subjects: *the kitchen*, *the dog*, and *the baby*.

▶ Subjects at different places in a sentence

You can see that each of the following sentences begins with an introductory *phrase* (that is, a group of words *without* a working verb). Then comes the subject and its verb:

> Three hours after sunrise, **Bill** *spotted* the heron.

> Despite the rain and cold, **Bill** *had waited* by the stream.

> By a roundabout route, **Bill** *returned* to the town.

In the following sentences, the usual order is reversed in order to give impact. The subject of each verb, therefore, sits right at the end of the sentences:

> Out of the cave, *crawled* **Brian**.

> Beside the motorbike, *stood* **its owner**.

▶ The subject of a passive verb

You may remember passive verbs from chapter 1. Most verbs are active. This means that, as I keep saying, the subject is the person or thing *doing* the verb. In the case of passive verbs, something is being done *to* the subject. Let's go back to the sentences I used in chapter 1:

> **I** *was bitten* by the dog.

> **I** *bit* the dog.

It's easy to see that, in the second sentence, *I* is the subject of the verb *bit*. Biting is what *I* did. It's not so easy to see that *I* is also the subject of the first sentence. You might assume that, since the dog did the biting, it is he (or she) who is the subject. But the *focus* of the sentence is on *I*, and *was bitten* is a *passive* form of the verb *to bite*.

Similarly, in *both* the next two sentences, the subject is *Polly* even though, in the second sentence, the alien wins:

> **Polly** *ate* a toffee apple.

> **Polly** *was eaten* by a creature from outer space.

In the next two sentences, however, the subject of the first is *Max*, and the subject of the second is *the referee*:

> **Max** *was shouted* at by the referee.

> **The referee** *shouted* at Max.

The verb in the first sentence is passive, and the one in the second sentence is active.

You could make the point that it is Max's experience that is more important than the referee's in both sentences here. The second sentence could have come from a newspaper report on a footballer. In this particular sentence, however, the verb is active: the referee is doing the shouting. At this point in our imaginary news report, it is the referee's action that is the focus of attention.

You can see from this that each sentence has to be analysed *by itself* in order to find the subject of its verb. We can't rely on surrounding information in order to find this out.

► 'Extended subjects'*

It often happens that a *group* of words functions as the subject of the main verb in a sentence. This group will often begin with an *ing* word (that is, a verb ending in *ing*) or with the word *that*. Here are some examples:

Planning a holiday *is* fun.

To worry about exams *is* a waste of time.

Collecting wood for the fire *took* a long time.

Looking after the horse *was* Sid's responsibility.

That Patrick was in two minds *was* clear from the way he hesitated.

That nations must co-operate in order to achieve lasting peace *is* obvious.

You'll probably have noticed that each of those particular subjects actually contains either an *ing* word or an infinitive or even a fully working verb. Don't worry about this at the moment. You'll find more information on this kind of thing in chapter 8.

In each case here, we can check out the **subject** by asking ourselves a question. *What* was it, for example, that *took a long time*? It was *Collecting wood for the fire*. *What* was *Sid's responsibility*? It was *Looking after the horse*, of course.

ACTIVITY 5

Underline the subjects of all verbs in the following sentences:

1 Carl won the race.
2 After breakfast, Ron did the washing up.
3 Over the hill, rode the cowboy.
4 Pam was given a bonus by her boss.

---

* This term is my own. I made it up for convenience. You are unlikely to find it in any other grammar books.

5 Tomorrow, a belt of rain will cross the county and high winds will make driving difficult.
6 Every morning, Maxine was shown a different job in the greenhouses.
7 The children ate all the chocolate but the buns were left untouched.
8 To work at a satisfying job is a pleasure.

▶ Direct objects

You are probably used to using the word *object* to mean *objective*, as in *The object of reading this book is to improve my English.* In grammatical terminology, *an object is a person, animal or thing which is on the receiving end of the doing or having.*

A very simple sentence will be composed of a subject followed by a verb. Many sentences also contain an object:

Jack *hit* John.

I *threw* the ball.

Peter *owns* a Porsche.

Just as you can ask yourself who is doing the verb when you are looking for its subject, you can ask yourself who or what is, for example, being hit, thrown, or owned when you are endeavouring to find an object. The answers to those questions here are *John*, *the ball*, and *a Porsche*.

You can see that there's a *direct* relationship between Jack and John, and between I and *the ball*. In other words, in each sentence, the subject and object are directly related by the verb. The relationship between Peter and his *Porsche* is not *quite* so blatant as the relationship in each of the other two sentences, but it's pretty clear, all the same.

ACTIVITY 6

Put a ring around the objects in the following sentences:

1 The gangsters robbed the casino.
2 The police rounded up the suspects.

3 Gamblers clutched their winnings.
4 Rudy started a fight.
5 The newspapers reported the events.
6 The mayor wanted calm.

Many, many sentences have this basic structure of subject, verb, object.

▶ Indirect objects

In a sentence that includes an **indirect object** as well as a direct object, the relationship between this and the subject is clear, but is *not quite so close* as that of subject and direct object. For example:

> **Louise** *sent* <u>Father Christmas</u> <u>a letter.</u>
> **The children** *gave* <u>their teacher</u> <u>a present.</u>
> **Ron** *gave* <u>the dog</u> <u>a bone.</u>

direct objects	*indirect objects*
a letter	Father Christmas
a present	their teacher
a bone	the dog

If I write the sentences slightly differently, using the word 'to', you can see things more clearly:

> Louise sent a letter to Father Christmas.
> The children gave a present to their teacher.
> Ron gave a bone to the dog.

It is not always the case that the word *to* could be added. Sometimes the word *for* might be better. You just need to be aware of the distance between the subject and the indirect object.

ACTIVITY 7

Underline the indirect objects in the following sentences:

1 Jim will show you the photographs.
2 The schoolteacher set class IV an exercise.

3 The homoeopath gave her client some pills.
4 The Chancellor's budget will save us money.
5 The reflexologist gave me a treatment.

▶ The pronouns *I* and *me* as subject and object

When speaking and writing, in everyday situations, everyone automatically uses the words *I* and *me* correctly most of the time. The word *I* is always used for a subject and the word *me* for a direct or indirect object. The trouble usually arises whenever we have a friend or colleague with us. Look at the following sentences:

Subject

I	went to the cinema.
John	went to the cinema.
John and I	went to the cinema.

It's incorrect to say or write:

John and me went to the cinema

because *me* can only be used as an object, never as a subject.

More problems arise when there's a business associate involved or when we want to be sure to be polite. Many people are worried about sounding pushy and will say:

Mrs Smith and myself went to the meeting.

This is *not* what's needed. The correct way to say this is:

Mrs Smith and I went to the meeting.

Similar problems occur when the word *me* is used as an indirect object. This is how it should be done:

	Direct object		**Indirect object**	**Direct object**
1	John gave		me	the tickets.
2	John gave		Jane and me	the tickets.
3	John gave	the tickets	to Jane and me.	

Now look at this:

> Mrs Smith gave the report to myself.
> Mrs Smith gave the report to Jane and myself.

These sentences are not quite right. They should read:

> Mrs Smith gave the report to me.
> Mrs Smith gave the report to Jane and me.

You may have spotted that they are constructed in a similar way to sentence number 3 above.

You will hear the word *myself* misused all over the place. In truth, it has two specific uses:

1 It can be used to add stress to what we say:

> I'll do the job myself.
> I'll come to the meeting myself.

2 It can be used to show that the speaker is doing something *to* or *for* him- or herself. This is called a **reflexive** construction:

> I scratched myself.
> I gave myself a pat on the back.

In the second sentence, the word *myself* is acting as an indirect object. You may understand all this more easily if you compare the use of the word *myself* with that of the words *himself, herself* and *itself*:

> The runner hurt himself.
> Sally surprised herself.
> The cat licked itself.

By the way, there's a very simple way to check whether you need to use *I* or *me* when two people are involved: mentally omit the other person. You'd never say *Me went to the cinema* or *John gave I the tickets*. The correct constructions, therefore, are:

> John and I went to the cinema.

and

John gave Jane and me the tickets.

SUMMARY

A sentence must always:
• make sense
• contain a working verb
• contain a subject for that verb.

Note: An *ing* **verb** at the beginning of a sentence must have at least *two* parts.

- A **subject**: the person or thing doing the   doing
  being
  having.

- An **object**: the person or thing on the receiving end of the doing
  being
  having.

- An **indirect object**: the person or thing that is less close to the subject than the direct object.

- I   is a subject

- me   is an object

- myself   is used to add stress or in a reflexive construction (i.e. doing something to myself).

3 Perfect Punctuation

INTRODUCTION

At school, most of us were told that punctuation is used to show a reader where to take a breath. Well, there's some truth in that, but it's not the whole story, by any means. Punctuation is used in order to make our writing make sense. If you were to find a book that had no punctuation in it, you would find that it took much longer to read than usual and that some parts were difficult to understand. Look at this:

> knowledge of the identity of objects and features in the environment is obviously valuable to us not only does the apparent stability and permanence of most of them create a feeling of security it also enables us to react to them rapidly and appropriately we learn by experience what are the uses of houses shops and other buildings (M. D. Vernon, *The Psychology of Perception*, Penguin, 1971, p. 13)

Although this is well written and not too difficult to understand, it is much easier and quicker to read when punctuation is added:

> Knowledge of the identity of objects and features in the environment is obviously valuable to us. Not only does the apparent stability and permanence of most of them create a feeling of security; it also enables us to react to them rapidly and appropriately. We learn by experience what are the uses of houses, shops, and other buildings.

Now you may be wondering why I say that there's a difference between having your writing make sense and showing a reader where to breathe. Well, for a start, breathing is only important if you have to read aloud. When we're reading silently, we don't say to ourselves, "Ah, here's a full stop. I'll pause here", or "I'd better take a quick breath after this comma." When reading silently, your breathing is probably almost as regular as when you are asleep.

It's also interesting to note that when people do read aloud they often add more pauses than are indicated by the punctuation marks. Reading aloud is actually closer to talking; and when we talk, we start to use all sorts of extra tricks to make ourselves understood (as I showed in chapter 2). We vary the tone of our voices, pause on certain words for emphasis, constantly change the expressions on our faces, and may even start waving our arms around or moving about. All this will help a listener to understand what the words mean and even how we feel about what we are reading.

▶ Full stops*

If you have read chapter 2, you have already looked hard at how a sentence functions. Whenever I'm having to read something I find difficult to understand, I find that full stops can be incredibly helpful. From the beginning of a sentence, I run my eyes down the page until I come to the next full stop. This technique not only allows me to see how much information I need to take in one chunk, so to speak, but it also makes me feel more comfortable by showing me exactly where the next stopping-point is.

Then I can go back to the beginning of the sentence, reread it, and start finding out how its parts fit together and what it means. I can be confident that, when I have understood this sentence, I will have put in place the building block for understanding the next one, and in this way, I can slowly progress through a difficult piece of material.

Full stops are used to separate one statement (and any closely-related qualifications of it) from the next. For example:

> Sooner or later, most of us will want to learn to use the Internet.
> We will then have access to a vast range of information –
> ranging from courses offered by colleges in distant countries to
> extracts from encyclopaedias.

In the above, I have used a full stop to separate a sentence about the desire to use the Internet from one that states what this will mean to

---

* In American English, a full stop is called a *period*.

us. The desire and the effect are separate items. Each needs its own sentence.

Some people find it difficult to decide whether to use a comma or a full stop at any particular point. Actually, it is commas that are tricky, not full stops. Use commas only for the jobs outlined in the next section.

Before we move on, have a look at this extract from a student paper that assessed the possibilities for developing the college site where the writer's course was situated. Can you see where he needed to use a full stop?

> Many of the building systems which are on the market can be assembled within a matter of days, assuming that the groundwork is complete, they have no aesthetic value whatsoever, and although there are several such systems already on the site, more would undervalue what could, with a traditional building, create a more aesthetically pleasing work environment.

The comments on the speed of assembly of certain systems need to be separated from the comments on aesthetics. The extract needs a full stop after *complete.*

If you are in real difficulty over this, you might try what I once suggested to a student on an Access course: while drafting your essay, pretend that you are writing notes, and *leave a line between sentences.* This will force you to focus on keeping all the related parts of one sentence together – before you leave a gap. Your work will look a bit like a cooking recipe, but that is fine. You will soon become more proficient and then you won't need to bother with that kind of time-consuming exercise.

By the way, question marks or exclamation marks (see below) show, just like a full stop, that a sentence is complete.

▶ Commas

In order to get to grips with writing clear essays (and other material), you need to understand how commas function. But that's not the walkover it's often thought to be. Commas can be some of the trickiest things to get right.

When you are reading aloud, you'll be likely to pause briefly where you see a comma. Indeed, doing this will help your listeners understand what they're hearing. In fact, they have to be given quite a bit of help from your tone of voice and your emphasis, unless they have a copy of what you are reading in front of them. But when you're writing, you need to focus on putting in commas *solely in order to make your meaning clear*. As far as you are concerned, the readers can gasp, exhale, or hold their breath till they explode. All that concerns you is that there should be *no possible confusion* in what you have written.

I doubt, at this point, that you feel very much clearer, but don't worry. All will be revealed as we go along.

The simplest use of commas is for separating parts of a list:

> I went shopping and bought oranges, apples, pears and bananas.

You have probably been taught never to put a comma before the word *and*. So the punctuation in my example will look correct to you. Actually, the use of a comma before *and* is optional in a list. In a simple list like the one above, a comma is usually unnecessary; but it can be very useful in some cases in order to make it clear that the last two items in the list are quite separate.

As an example of this, look back for a moment at the quotation at the beginning of this chapter – the one about 'objects and features in the environment'. In the final sentence, the writer has put in a comma after the word *shops* and before *and*. This makes it clear that he is talking about three categories of buildings:

> houses
> shops
> other buildings

If he had omitted the comma after *shops*, it would be possible to read his sentence as talking about two categories:

> houses
> shops and other buildings

Do you see the difference? This may not seem a crucial distinction when we're talking of apples and oranges, but it can be really important when we're trying to distinguish between several complicated ideas. On the other hand, it might just be crucial with the fruit. Let's suppose that you are responsible for seeing that fruit and vegetables are packaged for distribution to retailers. You have left the following note for one of your team:

Please pack the oranges, apples, pears and bananas in boxes
from the store.

Your team member might have ended up with three boxes of fruit
when you had wanted four. A comma after *pears* would have made
your meaning clearer.

Commas are also used to separate descriptive words. For example,

Josh stared at the long, dark snake.

A single, shrill, piercing whistle was heard in the wood.

A comma is never used between the last descriptive word and the item
described.

When you get to grips with using commas, you'll find that
they are especially useful for *showing which groups of words fit together.*
It is very common for a sentence to begin with some introductory
words that set the scene, so to speak, but are not part of the
main statement. These can be marked off with a comma. In the
following example, the words *During the summer* fulfil this introductory
function:

During the summer, I am going to finish writing this book.

The crucial statement here is *I am going to finish this book.* It is a statement showing my clear intent. The publisher will be glad to know that
I intend to finish it before the summer ends, but even she will be most
concerned with the fact that I *am* going to finish it and have not given
up on the project.

We all know the next example:

Once upon a time, there lived an old king who had a lovely
daughter.

Those last two examples both relate to time. Here are two that relate
to place:

Underneath the cushion, I found the scissors I'd lost.

Beyond the town, the mud road stretched into the distance.

Commas are very useful for marking off all kinds of extra information from the main statement in a sentence:

> Stretching up on his hind legs, the dog peered over the low fence.

> Wrapped in blankets, the walking wounded shuffled to the helicopter.

Items of extra information can also be placed at the end of a sentence:

> Six boys were following the old man, jeering and catcalling.

> Meera used to make all the family's clothes, helped by her ancient sewing machine.

Look at the following two sentences and see if you can work out why I've used a comma in the first but not in the second:

> Maria went for a long walk, taking her lunch in a small bag.

> Maria went for a long walk across the fields to the river.

This is where the fun starts. Lots of people would want to put a comma in the second sentence as well as the first, but there's a subtle difference. You'll remember, from chapter 2, that a sentence makes a statement. It would actually be more correct to say that a sentence contains a statement. It may also contain other information as well. We saw that in those sentences above.

In the first sentence here, the statement is

> Maria went for a long walk

and the words

> taking her lunch in a small bag

give us some extra information. But in the second sentence, the statement is the whole sentence. The information on where Maria went is crucial to and part of that statement. Maria went only to the river. So no comma is needed. That sentence, as it is written at present, must be taken in one go.

But we could write this story slightly differently and so change the *emphasis*. We might say:

> Maria went for a long walk, slowly crossing the fields to the river.

Now *the fields* and *the river* become slightly less important. They are now extra information. The main feature of the sentence is the *long walk* and the itinerary takes second place. We might expect from this to be told in the next sentence that, after reaching the river, Maria carried on walking beyond it.

As we saw above, extra information can be put in different places in a sentence. Look at the following sentences:

> Swinging her bag in her left hand, Maria walked to the river.

> Maria walked to the river, swinging her bag in her left hand.

In both those sentences, the main statement is the same:

> Maria walked to the river.

The first sentence seems to me to contain a little suspense; the second seems solely descriptive. The position of the extra information merely varies the impact of the words. You can see that the difference is often quite subtle.

Let's look at how to put some *extra information in the middle of a sentence*:

> Maria, the girl who defied a brutal regime, walked to the river.

The main statement is still

> Maria walked to the river

but we now have some very interesting extra information about this person. When you put extra information in the middle of a sentence, always mark it off by commas – one before and one after.

I wonder if you agreed with me when I stated that *Maria walked to the river* was more important than the fact that she *defied a brutal regime*. In terms of Maria's whole life, a trip to the river seems a minor occurrence when compared with her bravery. But in this particular sentence, I'm *focusing* on the *walk* and I've made that the main statement of my sentence. Chapter 8 will give you more information on how to emphasize a particular item in a sentence.

Now look at the following examples:

> Paul, the man Josie had always loved, eventually married Catherine.

> I ran, stumbling and moaning, back to the hut.

> My dog Bruno, who barks ferociously, wouldn't hurt a fly.

Notice that, in each case, you could leave out the extra information and the sentence would still make perfect sense:

> Paul eventually married Catherine.

> I ran back to the hut.

> My dog Bruno wouldn't hurt a fly.

By putting commas around the extra information each time, I've demonstrated that I want my readers to concentrate on the other material in the sentences. For example, I want people to concentrate on Bruno's gentleness rather than his bark.

A common problem with commas

There's a problem with the following sentence that many people wouldn't spot. I wonder if you can see it:

> I went into town to do some shopping last week, it took me ages.

Now you already know that a sentence contains a statement. Well, sometimes it contains more than one. The statements here are:

> 1 I went into town to do some shopping last week

> 2 it took me ages

The problem here arises partly because we've all been told that the reason for using punctuation is to allow the reader to take a breath. So if I read that sentence aloud, pausing at the comma, anyone listening to me would understand perfectly. This is because they would hear two separate statements *as if these had been separated by a full stop*.

If there are two statements within one sentence, we need to know how the second relates to the first. In the section above, where extra information was added at the beginning, middle or end of a sentence, I used commas to mark it off and to show that it was not the most important thing in the sentence. But here we have two statements that appear to be equally important. I can sort out this problem by adding the word *and*:

> I went into town to do some shopping last week, and it took me ages.

Now it's ten to one that you're thinking, "That's wrong. When I was at school, we were told never to put a comma before *and*." Well, if you think back to the simple use of commas to separate items in a list – for example,

> apples, oranges and bananas

I think you'll see that it was here that the rule was drummed into you. That rule about not putting a comma before *and* only applied only to lists (and, as I said above, the practice is optional there anyway).

So let's look at some instances of sentences containing more than one important statement:

> Sue's grandma still rides a bike, she's ninety-three.

> I'm going to get rid of my car, it's so old it's falling apart.

> There was a queue at the traffic lights, I took a left turn to miss them.

All these sentences need sorting out because the meaning is not quite clear. It's *not* OK to separate two *equally* important statements with only a comma. There are two possible solutions. I could either replace the comma in each sentence with a full stop, or I could add a connecting word (or words) in each case to explain how the second statement relates to the first:

(a) Sue's grandma still rides a bike. She's ninety-three.

Here, the short sentences give impact to the statements.

(b) Sue's grandma still rides a bike, *even though* she's ninety-three.

This gives the information in a slightly more gentle fashion. In this sentence, it would probably be better to omit the comma altogether. Similar things can be done with the other sentences above:

(a) I'm going to get rid of my car. It's so old it's falling apart.
(b) I'm going to get rid of my car *because* it's so old it's falling apart.

(a) There was a queue at the traffic lights. I took a left turn to miss them.
(b) There was a queue at the traffic lights, *so* I took a left turn to miss them.

Can you spot the problems with commas in the following piece of student writing? Claire has written a poignant description of a time when she had to travel without her children:

> *It felt most strange watching my children wave me off, they looked so small standing on the vast now empty platform. As the train pulled away, they had tried to keep up by running alongside, they were aware that this was not possible but had tried anyway.*

In the first two lines, Claire's writing would gain strength from separating the two statements with a full stop. Short sentences can have impact and would work particularly well here because both statements about the children would then be emphasized, and we would be forced to take the information more slowly and so to empathize even more with the writer.

There's also a problem with the comma after *alongside* because there is an equally important statement on each side of it. Because of the length of this sentence, I think that Claire could improve her piece with a full stop here too.

Commas need very careful handling. A good rule of thumb is: *never use one unless you know exactly why you are doing so.* They are better omitted than used incorrectly.

ACTIVITY 1

Add commas, where necessary, to the following sentences:

1 Marian has travelled in France Spain Australia India and the USA.
2 We were watched by a lean ageing kangaroo.
3 After two weeks on buses and trains it was a relief to smell sea air.
4 Jason our guide walked fast and spoke little.
5 Air disasters it is well known are fewer than accidents on the roads.
6 Taking a foreign holiday despite problems with accommodation currency and language can be a liberating experience.
7 Day after day the grey rocks dotted here and there with small plants formed a backdrop for our trek.
8 Taking a foreign holiday can be a liberating experience.

▶ Semicolons

A semicolon is usually thought of as indicating a longer pause than that given by a comma. Well, that's partly true, but a rather better definition would be to say that it indicates a slightly shorter pause than a full stop.

The reason for turning the definition around is because it now carries an implicit reminder that when you use a semicolon, whatever you write on *each* side of it *must* function *as if it were a separate sentence*. That means that there must be a clear statement, including a subject and working verb on *each* side of the semicolon – like this:

Many Westerners **like** Eastern food; Indian restaurants and take-aways, for example, **have opened** in most British towns.

The working verb in the first statement is *like* and its subject is *Many Westerners*. In the second statement, the working verb is *have opened* and the subject is *Indian restaurants and takeaways.*

The use of semicolons is generally a matter of choice. They could almost always be replaced by full stops without harming the sense of what you write. Their usefulness lies in allowing you to keep within one sentence statements that are very closely related to each other. Like all other punctuation marks, they are used to assist meaning.

Semicolons can also be used in certain lists:

> I went shopping for apples, pears and bananas; flour, sugar and spaghetti; milk, cheese and yoghurt.

In this case, the semicolons separate one *type* of item from another type.

Semicolons can also be very useful for separating sections in a long sentence where

> (a) the sentence follows a pattern

and

> (b) you need to use commas within the separate sections.

For example,

> It was decided that a steering group should be formed, consisting of six members; that publicity, particularly via the local media, would be essential; and that a celebrity, preferably from TV, should be approached to be patron of the new society.

The pattern shows up clearly if I make the sentence into a table:

It was decided:	that a steering group should be formed ...
	that publicity ... would be essential
	that a celebrity ... should be approached ...

You'd need those semicolons, however, only when the sections themselves contain commas. The following sentence needs none:

> It was decided to form a steering group consisting of six

members, to seek publicity via the media, and to approach a TV celebrity for the position of patron.

ACTIVITY 2

In the following paragraph, it would be possible to replace **two** of the full stops with semicolons. Which two? Why?

Many people have strong opinions on the use of the private car. Some feel that it has liberated the individual and brought with it a new level of personal freedom. Others feel that the threat to the environment posed by fuel emissions must be curtailed. Governments can find themselves caught between these mutually exclusive standpoints. They don't want to be seen as autocratic and reactionary. At the same time, they are aware of global warming and of the fact that they are likely to be held responsible for environmental decline.

▶ Colons

Colons are handy for introducing lists:

I bought various items at the hardware store: nails, paint, brushes, a screwdriver, a hammer and some string.

They are also useful for introducing quotations, like this:

When Hamlet sees his mother die and realises the poisoned drink was meant for him, his response is swift:

O villainy! Ho! Let the door be lock'd.
Treachery! Seek it out.

If you look through this book, you will see that I've used colons a great deal for introducing instructions and explanations. Here is another example:

Make the sauce as follows: first melt an ounce of butter in a saucepan, then add a tablespoon of flour, and finally slowly add about half a pint of liquid.

There's a further use for colons in which they indicate a kind of balance between the two halves of a sentence, and in which the second half elaborates on the first. For example,

> The unrest seems to have been caused by three specific factors: the invention of new machinery that put many people out of work, the rising cost of food, and an unusually hard winter.

> I'm an optimist: my glass is generally half full rather than half empty.

> Television can be seen as having both positive and negative aspects: it is an unrivalled means of communication, but it can ultimately dull the responses of viewers.

▶ Brackets

Brackets can be used in order to add extra information in a rather similar way to the use of a pair of commas:

> Dale (who was always a difficult child) refused to go to school until he had been bribed with the promise of hard currency.

Brackets can also contain information that qualifies the remainder of the sentence:

> Britain's Queen Victoria was (in most respects) a strong woman.

Or they can add extra information which, while being important, does not strictly fit into the sentence as it stands:

> Queen Victoria (1819–1901) ruled during a period of industrial expansion.

> In my garden (I have a small plot at the side of the house) I grow vegetables and roses.

You will notice that the first two examples can be read straight through, including what is in the brackets, without harming the sense. The third example does not read quite so smoothly, and the section in brackets in the fourth sentence is grammatically quite separate from the main sentence. All of these are acceptable, but the first two are rather neater than the others.

▶ Dashes

These can be used in a similar way to brackets to add a separate piece of information to a sentence. When this information is in brackets it can seem to be cut off from the rest of the sentence. When you use a pair of dashes, you'll need to make sure that whatever lies between them fits into your sentence smoothly and grammatically, like this:

> Britain's Queen Victoria was – in most respects – a strong woman.

A dash can sometimes be particularly handy, however, for adding a piece of information at the *end* of a sentence *without* having to fit it carefully to the grammar and sense of the sentence itself. This use of a dash can be dramatic, but if you do it too often in essays, your work may look slipshod. Keep it up your sleeve for occasional use only. It's done like this:

> Joan was always on hand to help with the decorating – she's a star.

> There were a number of pieces missing from the puzzle – sixteen, in fact.

Always leave a space before and after a dash so that it won't be confused with a hyphen.

▶ Hyphens

These look similar to dashes, but they are actually shorter and are used quite differently. There is no space between a hyphen and the letters on either side of it. Hyphens can be a bit tricky because of the number of different rules on how and where to use them. Their use is subject to change over time, and, in general, they are being used less frequently nowadays. The British tend to use more of them than the Americans. For example:

non-standard	British English
nonstandard	American English

Sometimes, two words that began life separately are then written with a hyphen and finally come to be known as just one word. For example, the word *today* was once written *to-day*. Language changes all the time – new words come into use and certain words fall out of use, sometimes becoming so old-fashioned that they don't seem relevant to our lives any more. The whole world is currently in a period of great change. While this is interesting, it can result in many more language changes than we feel comfortable with.

Hyphens have three uses:

1 at the end of a line where there's no space for an entire word

For example:

The British comedian Eddie Izzard has suggested that when your cat is sitting behind your couch and purring, the situation may not be as innocent as it sounds. Although you may think your moggy is peacefully resting, he may actually be drilling. "Some of them go down as much as forty feet," he said.

When splitting a word in this manner, aim to break it smoothly in relation to both the sound and the appearance of the word. It would have looked a bit strange if I had broken *peacefully* as *pea-cefully*.

2 in words that are regularly written with a hyphen

For example:

book-keeping
re-export

In both of these words, the hyphen is used to avoid awkwardness with a double letter. This is often a clue as to whether or not you need to use a hyphen. But it's not a hard and fast rule; many people now write *cooperate* rather than *co-operate*.

3 for joining two or more words to make a new one

For example:

> a sky-blue dress
> a half-eaten sandwich

We often want to do this when describing things. Without the hyphen, it must be possible for both words to be *separately* applicable to the word being described. If I had written

> A sky blue dress

I would have said something rather different from what I said when I used a hyphen. I would have implied that the dress was both *sky* and *blue*. The first of these is clearly nonsense.

If I omit the hyphen from my description of the sandwich, I would imply that it was both *half* a sandwich *and* an *eaten* one – which also sounds pretty silly, because if it was *eaten*, it wasn't there at all.

If you say aloud to yourself the examples of the dress and the sandwich, you'll probably notice that, when we combine two words to describe something, we run them together and speak them more quickly than when we are using them separately. Thinking about the sound can be a rather useful way to help to decide whether to join with a hyphen words that we often think of as separate.

Omission of necessary hyphens can clearly cause quite serious problems of meaning. For all examples except the joining of two words to make a new and imaginative description, it is often best to check the dictionary. It's also a good idea to memorize any hyphenated words which are specific to your own subject and which you will need to use frequently.

▶ Exclamation marks

Probably the best advice here is: don't use exclamation marks, except when writing dialogue in stories. It is usually felt that we should demonstrate important points through our writing itself and not rely on exclamation marks to do the work. In fact, these marks are actually frowned upon when they appear in essays because they indicate strong emotion, and the best essays are generally logical and unemotional.

Exclamation marks are, however, very handy in stories for showing when someone is shouting or screaming, like this:

"Let go!" yelled Mick.

or

"Fire!" shouted the Principal from the staff room.

or

"Help!" screamed Pat.

It's also fine to use exclamation marks in letters to friends where there are no rules to worry about. Most people do this from time to time. One year, all my letters to distant friends contained exclamation marks. I had been having a particularly difficult time decorating my kitchen, and I wrote about both the difficulties and the cost:

> *The week when I had to use the steam stripper to remove*
> *six layers of wallpaper from the wood panelling was, of course,*
> *the week of the heat-wave. Now I know what a Turkish bath is*
> *like! And the cost of decorating that one wall was, would you*
> *believe, £70!*

It's also important to remember not to use a full stop as well as an exclamation mark. Only *one* punctuation mark is used at a time.

▶ Question marks

These are sometimes called 'interrogation marks' – particularly in American English.

The main thing here is to remember to use them. It's amazing how easy it is to forget to use a question mark after a question. The lack of one is, however, horribly apparent to a reader.

As with an exclamation mark, never use a full stop as well as a question mark. Don't forget, however, that a question mark always terminates a sentence, so you need to follow it with a capital letter.

Questions can be a real problem in essays and other formal documents. Difficulties can also arise in reporting questions that other people have asked. You will find a section on how to deal with this in chapter 6.

▶ Apostrophes

Apostrophes have two jobs to do – and these are quite distinct. One is to show when there is a letter (or letters) *missing* from a word. This will usually be in conversational speech or informal writing. This is called **contraction**. The other is to show when something *belongs* to someone or something. This is called **possession**.

Contraction
This is really simple. In the following sentence, I have used an apostrophe to show that the letter *o* is missing:

I didn't get where I am today by ignoring apostrophes.

If I had written this in full, I would have put *I did not get* ... .

The following table gives a selection of the kind of examples that are found in everyday speech:

You'll find this easy.	You will
We *won't* be long.	will not
I *wouldn't* do that if I were you.	would not
He'll be here next week.	He will
They'll do their best.	They will
Aren't you clever!	Are not*
I *wasn't* at work today.	was not

Possession
This is where you may be having difficulties. You probably have some vague memories from school about putting an apostrophe before or after an *s* but it's ten to one that you can't remember why or when; and a lot of people have become so muddled as to think that every plural word needs an apostrophe. That is certainly not the case.

Because there has been such confusion over possession, I'd like to suggest that you ignore that old *s* rule and use a rule that is new and

---

* This is no longer used. The remark, "Are not you clever?" would sound odd and very old-fashioned.

simpler. All you need to remember is to put an apostrophe *immediately after the owner*. Take the following sentence:

> The dog's tail got caught in the door.

Whenever you write down something where possession seems to be involved, you just ask yourself one simple question: who is the owner? In this case, we need to ask: who owns the tail? The answer is the dog. So you put the apostrophe immediately after *dog*. You will automatically have written this down with *s* because we hear it and say it automatically.

There may be some examples that you feel are tricky, but if you apply the new rule, you will find that it really is very simple:

> 1 We could see the elephants trunks waving over the wall.
>
> Q Who owns the trunks?
> A The elephants

So the apostrophe goes immediately after *elephants*:

> We could see the elephants' trunks waving over the wall.
>
> 2 Peoples tastes differ.
>
> Q Who owns the tastes?
> A People

So the apostrophe goes immediately after *People*:

> People's tastes differ.

If you try to *combine* this rule with the old *s* rule, you will confuse yourself. Make a clean break, apply the new rule, and, I promise you, you can't go wrong.

By the way, if you have ever worried about using an apostrophe for *Mr Smith* or *Mrs Jones*, the following should help:

> I borrowed old Mr Smith's lawnmower last week. Then I lent it to Mrs Jones' aunt. The Smiths' son was furious, but the Joneses' daughter thought it was all very funny.

Smith is an easy name to cope with as it doesn't end in *s*. Where a name does end in *s*, it may sound a bit odd to add another one to indicate possession. All we need is an apostrophe – *Mrs Jones' aunt*. The name *Jones* is changed to *Joneses* (showing that the word is plural) when we want to talk about the family. An apostrophe is added to this if, and only if, we want to indicate possession *at the same time*:

the Joneses' daughter   the daughter of Mr and Mrs Jones

It's and *its*
The first of these is a **contraction** and the second shows **possession**. There's just one problem here: how do we remember which is which?

Well, there's a very simple solution. Each time you write *its*, you just ask yourself, "Do I mean *it is*?" (or, occasionally, *it has*). If the answer is "Yes", you put in an apostrophe and move on. If "No", you just move on anyway. The important thing here is not to hesitate and start wondering if you really have got it right. That will only lead to confusion. Just ask yourself the question and act decisively on the answer.

SOME EXAMPLES OF *IT'S* AND *ITS*
Contraction

It's raining.	*It is* raining.
It's not often you see a gnu.	*It is* not often you see a gnu.

The word *it's* is used in conversation in stories and in informal writing such as letters to friends. I've used it a good deal in this book because I didn't want to sound formal. In your essays, however, stick to writing *it is* because that is the correct form for academic writing.

Possession
The word *its* (without any apostrophe) is one of a group of words that deal with possession. Some of these also end in *s*, but none of them uses an apostrophe. The others are: *my, his, her, our, ours, your, yours, their, theirs*. They are called **possessive adjectives**, but it's not necessary to remember that term. Here is the word *its* used to show possession:

The cat ate *its* dinner.
The ceremony moved towards *its* ending.
The storm was at *its* height.

The words *its* and *it's* look very similar; but now that you can see clearly that their meanings are, in fact, very different, you'll quickly learn to use them accurately.

ACTIVITY 3

Add apostrophes, where necessary, to the following sentences:

1 Its only when I laugh that it hurts.
2 Its a lovely day today.
3 Johns fathers got his brothers coat.
4 When its raining, that dog always stays in its kennel.
5 Its easy to see how the cat shut its paw in the Browns gate.
6 The hyenas eyes were visible in the bushes everywhere we looked.

▶ Abbreviations

Until quite recently, items like *VIPs* and *the 1990s* were always given an apostrophe (*VIP's*, *1990's*). Now, however, it has become usual to omit the apostrophe. I think this is neater.

As a general rule, use an apostrophe only when you are certain you know where it goes. An apostrophe in the wrong place looks much worse than one omitted.

SUMMARY

• a full stop is used to	separate one statement and its closely related information from another
• a comma is used to	separate items in a list
	separate two or more words used descriptively
	separate any two statements that are linked by *and, so, but, because*, etc.
	mark off extra information from the main statement:

	at the beginning or end of a sentence
	in the middle of a sentence – two commas
• a semicolon is used to	keep two statements closer than when using a full stop
	Note: whatever is on *each* side must have its own subject and working verb
• a colon is used to	introduce a list, an explanation, or a quotation
	demonstrate balance between two statements
• brackets are used to	incorporate extra information
• dashes are used to	incorporate extra information:
	in the middle of a sentence (two dashes)
	at the end of a sentence
• a hyphen is used to	split a word at the end of a line
	show the separate parts of certain words
	join words to make a new word
• an exclamation mark is used to	demonstrate passion in speech
• a question mark is used to	indicate a question
• an apostrophe is used to	show contraction (a letter or letters missing) or possession
• **its** is used to	show possession
• **it's** is used to	stand instead of *it is* or *it has*

4 More Parts of Speech

INTRODUCTION

The information contained in this chapter will be optional for many people, although all students who are taking English courses will definitely need to be aware of it.

In traditional grammar, all the words we ever use (well, very nearly all) fall into one of eight groups. These groups are called parts of speech – or, sometimes, word classes. Some grammarians now define some extra categories, but you need not worry about those in order to have a good basic understanding of how parts of speech function.

The good news is that, if you've read the chapter on verbs, you already understand one of the parts of speech. Of the other seven, four are important and worth learning about, but unless you plan to study linguistics (or a related subject) you can ignore the other three. The ones I'll look at closely are: nouns, pronouns, adjectives and adverbs.

▶ Nouns

In a nutshell, nouns are **words for people, places and things**:

People	Places	Things
boy	New York	table
girl	Adelaide	car
Mrs Thatcher	Japan	clock
Buddha	Niagara Falls	milk
Mick Jagger	St Paul's Cathedral	computer
Bill Gates	the French Riviera	grass

The **names of animals, birds, insects and sea creatures** are also nouns:

dog	eagle	beetle	whale
cat	sparrow	bee	seal
lion	duck	moth	octopus

The **names of government departments, companies, corporations and shops** are nouns too; and so are **brand names**:

Berkshire County Council	Marks and Spencer	Coca-Cola
United States of America	the Catholic Church	Nescafé
Microsoft	McDonald's	Levis
Toshiba	Debenhams	Porsche
Barclays Bank	Macy's	Persil
Live Aid	The Foreign Office	Tesco

Seasons, periods of time and **words relating to weather** are also nouns:

spring	hour	snow
summer	minute	sunshine
autumn	month	wind
winter	century	rain

Here are some sentences with the nouns highlighted in bold type:

Joan threw the **ball** across the **garden**.
Toshiba are building a new **factory** in **Wales**.
The French are known for good **food**.
The **moon** and **stars** shine brightly on a clear **night**.

One way of understanding nouns is to remember that *it is usually possible to see and/ or touch them*. You can put some nouns in your pocket, eat some for breakfast, meet some for a drink, read about them in the paper, or possibly bump into them.

ACTIVITY 1

Underline the nouns in the following sentences:

1 Mrs Steele sent a letter to the Queen.
2 Bees make honey.

3 Carlos has been living in France for six years.
4 Mary wanted a bike.
5 Julius Caesar ruled in Rome.

The whole category of nouns can also be divided into two groups – into what are known as **concrete and abstract nouns**. Concrete nouns are the ones we have already been looking at. These are the ones that can be seen, touched, or found in some form. **Abstract nouns, as the name suggests, are things that it is not possible to find**. Below are some examples of the two types:

Abstract	*Concrete*
beauty	flower
education	book
war	gun
kindness	gift
love	ring
crime	thief
sadness	tears
religion	church

Notice that each concrete noun above is related to the corresponding abstract noun on its left.

Abstract nouns are things that we often talk about but we wouldn't be able to see. They are usually generalized ideas or emotions. Concrete nouns, on the other hand, can be found somewhere – even if it takes some searching.

So things like the heart and lungs are concrete rather than abstract nouns because, in an operation, they are visible. Ghosts, too, surprisingly, are concrete. If they exist, they are visible and very specific. On the day that I see one, I shall be able to describe it in detail. Air and other gases are concrete too (even though we can't usually see them), because they can be measured. We could obtain a jar of hydrogen, so it's not abstract.

Abstract nouns can only be talked about – never found. We can see a beautiful painting or person, but we can't find a piece of beauty; we can find students and lecturers and universities, but we can't get hold of a piece of education.

ACTIVITY 2

Underline the concrete nouns and put a ring round the abstract nouns in the following:

1 Water is essential for life.
2 Exercise is important for health.
3 The atmosphere in the bar was dense with smoke.
4 The monk had great understanding.
5 The members of the committee talked endlessly about strategy.
6 Paul was studying philosophy.

▶ **Pronouns**

Pronouns save an awful lot of time. They are used *in place of nouns*. It would be both boring and time-consuming to have to write the following:

> Jack was born in Toronto, but soon Jack's parents moved to Britain. Jack went to school in Huddersfield. Jack worked in a local garage for five years and then Jack studied design at evening classes. Jack has now started Jack's own business, making greeting cards.

Obviously, we all use pronouns all the time. If you look back to the section where I set out verbs, you will see that they follow the same pattern as the list of *personal pronouns* below – from first-person singular to third-person plural:

I/me	we/us
you	you
he/him/she/her/it	they/them

Pronouns are so simple that I'm not going to include an activity on them here. But there is one particularly important thing you need to know about using them. When you use a pronoun, make sure that you have used the relevant noun first and that the pronoun lies fairly close to it.

Can you see what's wrong with this extract from Derek's essay?

> *In the Neolithic era, many tools were already in use and archaeological remains can tell us much about the undertakings of daily life. They were able to make stone tools for their agricultural needs.*

When we are reading, we need to be absolutely sure of the noun to which any pronoun refers. Otherwise, things may not make sense. The rule is that a pronoun will stand for the closest previous noun. Generally speaking, as readers, we automatically work out which noun that is without thinking. But as writers, we need to be in the habit of making sure that we've got things correct so that there can never be any confusion.

In this extract from Derek's essay, I have to look for a plural noun because he has used the plural pronoun *They*. The closest plural noun is *undertakings*. Derek's second sentence would not make sense, however, if I were to substitute *undertakings* for *They*. What he actually meant was:

> People were able to make stone tools for their agricultural needs.

The noun *People* had not appeared anywhere, however, so the pronoun *They* couldn't refer to it and shouldn't, therefore, have been used at all. The sentence itself needed alteration.

The more complex the topics you write about, the more important it is to make sure that a pronoun lies close to the noun it stands for. If I write the following, it could become quite confusing:

> *Education is vital for all children, and financial survival is crucial for everyone, everywhere. Governments are morally bound to provide it.*

The word *it* is singular, and I had intended that it should refer to *Education*; but the closest singular noun is *survival* (modified by the adjective *financial*). Now *financial survival* is, of course, crucial for everyone. So anybody reading what I wrote is likely to assume that I meant that it is essential for governments to make sure that individuals are given the means for *financial survival*. Obviously, *financial survival* is likely to be largely dependent on education; but my intended focus on the importance of education itself is quickly becoming obscured. What's happened here is that I have not fully explained what I meant. I should have written something like this:

> *Education is vital for all children and governments are morally bound to provide it. Without education, a young person has less chance of a job; without a job, he or she has little chance of financial survival.*

Now the word *it* clearly refers to *Education*, which is the closest previous singular noun.

There's also a further difficulty. In the following sentence, who do you think is referred to by the word *her*?

> Jack is Ruth's fiancé. He saw Ruth and Wendy coming up the path. He ran out and gave her a hug.

We would assume that, since Jack is engaged to Ruth, it was Ruth that he hugged. But *Wendy* is the closest noun to *her*. So maybe, for reasons we're not aware of, he hugged Wendy. Maybe she had just suffered a blow to her financial survival and needed cheering up. It just isn't clear from the way I've written the two sentences.

If you are writing an essay on one person – Hitler, for example – a good rule of thumb is to use the name at or near the beginning of each new paragraph and to continue with *he* throughout the paragraph. Of course, once you start mentioning different statesmen and other historical figures involved in situations with (or relating to) Hitler, you are back with the problem of having to check very carefully that any pronouns you use do actually stand for the person you had intended.

There are also some other types of pronoun, but it is not necessary for most people to worry about these. If you are really interested, you might like to know about *relative*, *possessive* and *demonstrative pronouns*:

Relative Pronouns
who, whom, that, which

Possessive Pronouns
my/mine, your/yours, his, hers, its, our/ours, their/theirs

Demonstrative Pronouns
this, these, that, those

► Adjectives

Adjectives are words that describe something. Look at the following sentence:

The old lady owned a beautiful red necklace.

There are three describing words in that sentence: *old*, *beautiful* and *red*. The first one tells us something about the lady. The other two tell us what the necklace looked like. If I had written merely

The lady owned a necklace

you wouldn't have had any idea what either she or it was like. But by using those adjectives, I've made the picture begin to come alive. You might start to wonder what the necklace was made of – coral, perhaps, or rubies.

Did you spot that *lady* and *necklace* are nouns? So **the rule is: adjectives describe nouns**. In the following sentences, I've underlined the adjectives:

There was an <u>enormous</u> dog in the office.
John's <u>crazy</u> mother brought a <u>large</u>, <u>fat</u> hen to church.
Old Pat owned a <u>noisy</u> parrot.

Adjectives are also used to describe pronouns:

He was <u>hot</u>.
They are <u>happy</u>.

You can see from the last two examples that adjectives can be used in a simple way with parts of the verb *to be*. Here are some more examples:

The children are <u>hungry</u>.
The dress was <u>expensive</u>.
The sun is <u>hot</u>.

▶ Adverbs

Now that you know that adjectives describe nouns, you may have guessed that *adverbs are used to describe verbs*. They show us how things are done. The good news here is that the vast majority of adverbs end in *ly* so they are usually very easy to spot. They are formed by putting *ly* on the end of an adjective. Look at the following sentence:

Sarah walked home <u>slowly</u>.

You'll remember that most verbs are action words (and that every sentence must have a verb). The verb here is *walked*. The word *slowly* tells us *how* Sarah walked, and gives us the beginning of a visual picture. While you are practising spotting the difference between adjectives and adverbs, it's a good idea to ask yourself:

(a) Which word is being described?
(b) What part of speech is that word?

If I were new to this, I'd be saying to myself, "Which word does *slowly* describe? Is it *Sarah*? Well, she is going *slowly*. But that doesn't quite seem quite right. I can't say that Sarah is *slowly*. Let's try *walked*. Ah yes, that fits." If I ask myself the question, "How did Sarah walk?", I'm bound to come up with the answer *slowly*.

You can see the difference between adjectives and adverbs in these two sentences:

My room is tidy.
I have arranged my room tidily.

In the first sentence, the word *tidy* describes the word *room*, which is a noun. So *tidy* must be an adjective. In the second sentence, the word *tidily* tells you how I *arranged* the place. The word *arranged* is a verb. It tells us about an action. So *tidily* must be an adverb because it describes a verb.

There are a few adverbs that are not quite so easy to spot, but they work in just the same way as the *ly* adverbs, for example:

The boy ran <u>fast</u>.
We worked <u>hard</u>.

The word *fast* tells us how the boy *ran*. The word *hard* tells how we *worked*. The words *ran* and *worked* are both verbs, of course.

If we want to be a bit more academic about this, we can use the term *modify* instead of *describe*. It's a little more precise because, rather than confining the job solely to describing, it implies that the effect of a particular word is *changed* slightly.

As well as modifying verbs, adverbs can also modify adjectives and other adverbs – though it's less important for you to remember this. If you want to pursue this one, take a few minutes to see if you can work out how adjectives and adverbs function in the following sentence:

> The soldier will probably easily outrun his very heavily loaded colleague.

If we start at the end of the sentence, we can see that *colleague* is a noun. The word *loaded* describes it, and so is an adjective. This is modified by the word *heavily* which must therefore be an adverb. This, in turn, is modified by *very*, which must then be another adverb. The verb is *will outrun* and it is modified by *easily*, which is therefore yet another adverb. Finally, the word *probably* modifies *easily* so that, too, is an adverb. I'll list them for clarity:

Nouns	*Verb*	*Adjective*	*Adverbs*
soldier	will outrun	loaded	probably
colleague			easily
			very
			heavily

There are also a few words which are adverbs although you might not, at first glance, expect them to be, for example:

> how, where, when, why

In the following sentences, each of the above words modifies a verb. The verbs are in bold type.

1 How **is** John?
2 Where **is** Joan's coat?
3 When **did** you **buy** your car?
4 Why **was** Roy **laughing**?

Notice that, in sentences 3 and 4, the verbs (which, in those sentences, have two parts) are split apart.

The words *here* and *there* are also adverbs. Again, the verbs are in bold type:

1 Please **put** your boots here.
2 I've **left** my rucksack there.

ACTIVITY 3

Underline the adverbs in the following:

1 I felt I'd managed the first essay beautifully.
2 Slowly and silently, the cat crept through the grass.
3 I finished my lunch quickly.
4 Cheetahs can run fast.
5 Jason has worked harder and harder throughout the year.
6 The athlete jumped high.
7 Josh had a green jacket that he loved dearly.
8 Dan answered the question rather rashly.

▶ Conjunctions

A conjunction is a word that connects either two other words or whole constructions such as phrases or clauses (see chapter 8):

and	because
but	if
or	although

Here are a couple of examples used in sentences:

I'll come down the pub **if** John gets home early.
I'll come down the pub, **although** I'm short of cash.

▶ Prepositions

Prepositions have a number of uses. The main function of a preposition is to appear before a noun or pronoun and link this word in some way to another part of the sentence. Examples of prepositions are:

at, from, of, through, without, during, for

Here are some of them used in sentences:

1 I left my umbrella **at** the hospital.
2 I had a present **from** my aunt.
3 I've come **without** my diary.
4 I like using an old spoon **for** planting bulbs.

Perhaps the most common use of prepositions is to show the position of something in relation to something else. Look at the following sentence:

I put the saucepan **on** the cooker.

I could substitute a number of words for the word *on* and still make perfect sense (though my statements might not be true in relation to my kitchen):

in, beside, under, near

▶ Interjections

These are very often one-word shouts, such as:

Hey! Oops! Bother! Ouch! Ugh!

They are also one-word greetings (or the opposite), such as:

Hello! Hi! Cheers! Goodbye!

▶ The cat sat on the mat

You can use this very basic sentence as a way of remembering the four main parts of speech: nouns, verbs, adjectives and adverbs. I've set out a plan and added other words to help make the grammar clear and fix it in your mind.

You'll probably find it easiest to focus on one line at a time. You might like to take a ruler or a piece of paper and place it so that you can see just the first line, and then slide it down each time you are ready to look at the next one.

adjective	noun	verb	adverb		adjective	noun
The	cat	sat		on the		mat.
The black	cat	sat		on the	red	mat.
The frisky	kitten	sat	slyly	on the	new	rug.
The thin	Siamese	squatted	shyly	on the	Turkish	carpet.

If you've been really keen, you might have realized that *on* is a preposition. The word 'the' is what is called a **determiner**, but it's not necessary to remember that.

SUMMARY

► Nouns
people, places, things, brand names, shops, companies and any other observable items
  concrete nouns: all the above
  abstract nouns: concepts and feelings (that can be spoken of but not found)

► Pronouns
words that stand *instead* of nouns – e.g. *he, it, they*
a pronoun always relates to the closest previous noun (singular or plural respectively)

► Adjectives
words that **describe nouns** – e.g. *hot, happy*

► Adverbs
words (often ending in *ly*) that **describe verbs** – e.g. *quickly*

► Conjunctions
words that connect two other words, phrases or clauses – e.g. *and, but, so*

▶ Prepositions

link-words, often showing place – e.g. *on, at, beside*

▶ Interjections

shouts – e.g. "Bother!"
greetings – e.g. "Hello!"

5 Getting Conversation on Paper

INTRODUCTION

This chapter will cover both the rules for writing down the exact words that a person says – **direct speech** – and also how to write what is called **reported speech**, which is a way of recording that is useful for reports and is often used for committee minutes.

If you are studying English at any level you will need to be able to write direct speech accurately. On Access to Higher Education courses where English is a component of the course, you will probably be required to do some creative writing. You are likely to be asked to write a story, so you will need to be able to set down what your characters say. It's handy to be able to do this in letters, too.

The ability to write direct speech can also occasionally come in handy when writing essays. You may want to quote something said on TV or radio by a politician or academic. If you didn't catch the exact words, you might want to report on what he or she said. Either way, the information in this chapter will help you.

▶ Setting out direct speech

The term **direct speech** refers to the *actual words* that somebody speaks. The rules are really very straightforward. To begin with, everything that a person says is shown *inside* speech marks:

"A hurricane is coming."

There's no fixed rule on whether you use single or double marks. I use double so that I can keep speech distinct from quotes from books and articles – for which I use single marks (see chapter 7). In handwriting, the opening speech marks lean forwards and the closing ones lean back towards what has been said, but there is no need, when writing by hand, to put in those little blobs that sometimes show up in print. You can also see that the speech begins with a capital letter and ends with a full stop, just like any ordinary sentence. And notice, too, that the full stop is *inside* the speech marks: this is most important.

There are also hard and fast rules on how we show who is speaking:

The weather forecaster said, "A hurricane is coming."

Here, I've begun with the speaker followed by the word *said*. Then I've added a comma, and then I've carried on just as before. We can also do this the other way around. But here, there's an extra rule to remember:

"A hurricane is coming," said the weather forecaster.

This time, I had to put a comma at the end of the speech instead of a full stop, because I was going on to explain who spoke.

Here are two more examples of those two ways for showing who speaks:

Paul said, "Close the shutters."

"Close the shutters," said Paul.

Notice that whichever way I write this, the *punctuation mark* that follows the words spoken is *always inside* the speech marks.

If the hurricane has already arrived, however, Paul will not be speaking so calmly. We can show this in two ways: by the use of an exclamation mark to show that he's raising his voice, and by changing the word *said* to something more expressive:

Paul screamed, "Close the shutters!"

"Close the shutters!" screamed Paul.

Perhaps you've spotted a further problem here. I had to dispense with the comma following the word *shutters* in the second sentence because I wanted to use an exclamation mark to show that Paul is shouting. (By the way, it's *never* OK to use two punctuation marks beside each other.) An exclamation mark functions just like a full stop in that it marks the end of a sentence. So you might reasonably have expected the word *screamed* to begin with a capital letter. This, however, is the one exception to the rule on capitals following full stops, question marks, and exclamation marks. The word *said*, or any subsitute for it, always starts with a small letter when it follows somebody's actual words.

The following short exercise might help you to remember this one. Read that line about Paul aloud – with expression. You are likely to find that, however loudly you speak, you will run straight on to the words *screamed Paul*. You will not break at the exclamation mark. This may help you to remember that the *s* is small.

Here are some more examples:

Paul's grandfather yelled, "Get in the cellar!"

"Get in the cellar!" yelled Paul's grandfather.

Paul's mother shrieked, "Where's Magda?"

"Where's Magda?" shrieked Paul's mother.

You can see that a question mark, like an exclamation mark, functions similarly to a full stop by marking the end of a sentence.

There's just one more basic rule for setting out speech. Sometimes, when writing, we want to put *he said* or *she said* in the middle of what a person says, rather than at the beginning or the end. We do it like this:

"We'll sit tight," said Mr Webber, "until the worst is over."

You can see that we don't use a capital letter for the second half of the sentence. We are sometimes more likely to want to set out speech this way if we are writing a story. It allows us to use a variation on the *he said/she said* construction, and it can add a little tension. In this case, we have to wait until the end of the second half of the sentence to find out the full implication of what is being said. It can also slow things down and help to calm the atmosphere after a dramatic incident in which people are shouting.

The reason there is no capital for the word *until* in the example above is that it is *not* the beginning of a sentence. If we could actually hear the man speaking, we would hear:

"We'll sit tight until the worst is over."

The following example is constructed in the same way:

"There will be aid," a government spokeswoman said, "for the injured and for those whose property has been damaged."

Notice that, in each of these split items of speech, there are two commas – one after the first part of the speaker's sentence and one after the small section that shows the speaker's name with the word *said* – or *shrieked* or *yelled*.

At this point, I suggest you have a go at the following activity to practise these rules for speech. Refer to my examples while you do part A. Then see if you can do part B without looking anything up.

ACTIVITY 1

Add speech marks and *all* necessary punctuation and capital letters to the following sentences.

Part A
1 jack said my partner is expecting a baby
2 I was born in tunis said pierre
3 where is the post office asked the tourist
4 the toddler yelled i want an ice cream
5 that dog said john always disappears when I want to bath it
6 why asked tom have you put the beer under my bed

Part B
1 mary said the eggs are in the fridge
2 high tide will be at three this afternoon said the sailor
3 come back here yelled the policeman
4 sam asked politely how much extra will I have to pay
5 I havent laughed so much said ben since the chicken coop collapsed
6 the main difficulty explained the leader will be getting the tents across the river

Now you know the punctuation rules for conversation, we can look at how to set it out on the page. The usual rule here is: *new speaker, new line*. It's also usual to indent two or three spaces when a person starts to speak. Here's an example of how a newspaper might report speech from a hurricane incident (but note that newspapers don't always have enough space to stick to the rules all the time):

The first blast struck at two minutes past midnight. It was followed by three hours of hurricane force winds and torrential rain. A member of the Fire Service said,

"I've never seen anything like it."

There has been extensive damage. Many cars were blown into shop fronts in the main town square. A government spokeswoman stressed,

"There will be aid for the injured and for those whose property has been damaged."

There have been some lucky escapes, however. A farmer explained how his family, "huddled together", had sheltered in their cellar:

"I remembered," he said, "how we survived a hurricane in that cellar when I was a child."

The last item of speech here is preceded by a colon rather than the comma that you might have expected. That is because I have not used the word *said* at this point or any variation of it. I've used a rather indefinite phrase – *explained how*, together with part of the farmer's explanation. The colon, therefore, fits well here because it draws attention to the fact that what comes next is speech that will explain or develop what has just been written. The words *he said* can then be used in the middle of the farmer's speech to assist the flow of the sentence without the problem of repetition.

We've noticed that two words spoken by the farmer are included after *family* in the sentence that leads up to this final item of speech. Very short phrases like this can be included in a commentary without the need for a new line. You may be a bit confused over the position of commas here. If you think back to the section on commas in chapter 3, you'll see that *huddled together*, besides being a quote from what is clearly a longer section of speech, functions as an extra piece of information in the middle of a sentence. It therefore has a comma on each side of it – outside the speech marks.

If we wish, we can leave a word or two out as long as we indicate that something is missing by the use of dots:

"We are devastated here. ... I shall be visiting the injured all day,"
said a local priest.

Remember, finally, that the words inside speech marks are those that
were actually spoken. Well, yes, journalists do tend to give approximations of what was said, but there are occasions when doing that could
get *you* into hot water.

Totally accurate or not, here's an example of the film buff, Barry
Norman, using direct speech in a profile interview of the film director,
Alan Parker:

> One of Parker's strengths as a director is a sharp visual sense –
> the opening sequence of *Mississippi Burning*, the car chase in
> which three young Civil Rights workers are pursued by murder-
> ous rednecks, is simply pure cinema. And along with that goes a
> commendable refusal to come out of the same trap twice.
>
> "I try to do different things each time," he said. "I just think it
> keeps you creatively fresh. When I've finished a film I react
> against it, so I try not to repeat myself. But when you've done 12
> or 13 films you can't help but find yourself in a familiar alleyway,
> or up a staircase and you think 'Oh, I did this in *Angel Heart*', and
> that's really irritating. I feel I should always be going into areas
> where I haven't been before, because that makes me better as a
> film-maker."
>
> (Barry Norman, 'Rebel with a cause', *Radio Times,*
> Vol. 304, no. 3959, p. 54, 2000)

Notice, here, how the speaker actually quotes himself: he tells us
something that he repeatedly *thinks*. Since what Parker is saying is
already in speech marks, Barry Norman (the writer) uses single marks
for this thought. You might have expected the comma after *Angel Heart*
to come *inside* those single marks. In this case, however, that little
section is treated *as if it were a quote* (see chapter 7). So Norman does
not use the conventions of direct speech at that point.

ACTIVITY 2

Part A

The following is part of a report in the *Guardian* newspaper on the
cyclone in the Indian state of Orissa in November 1999. The report
refers to cyclone shelters built in Bangladesh. I have omitted all punc-

tuation. Copy out the extract, adding all necessary punctuation, including speech marks. Don't worry if you don't get this activity exactly right. The important thing is for you to have some practice in thinking out what to do.

> disaster experts now hope that the orissa cyclone will encourage the authorities to take similar safety measures it is only when you have a serious cyclone and people see bodies lying around that people get stirred into action says geoffrey dennis who heads the red cross in new delhi

Part B

Also from the *Guardian,* the following extract is from a report on the loss of control, by a farmer and farmworker, of a Land-Rover on a steep hill in Cornwall during bad weather. Again, all punctuation has been omitted here. Copy out and complete as you did for part A.

> both scrambled out unhurt as the vehicle careered downhill and could only watch in horror as it headed towards the converted former methodist chapel owned by the hawkins who are potters the possibilities were horrendous said mr sloman in shock after what he said had been a terrifying experience it was extremely wet and the vehicle aquaplaned on the grass lost traction and took off witnesses said the land rover bounced down the hillside like a tennis ball before plummeting through the slate roof of the pottery

▶ Indirect or reported speech

This section should be very useful if you have to take committee minutes or if you are planning to go into journalism. It's also handy for essays, articles and reports. It's particularly important for those who are studying for English exams. Before reading any further, you may need to check over the section on *tenses* in chapter 1 and/or the section on *pronouns* in chapter 4.

By using **reported speech**, we can do away with speech marks because we are going to make a statement *about* what someone said rather than using the exact words that were spoken. It's done like this:

Actual speech   Ron said, "The library is closed."
Reported speech Ron said that the library was closed.

As you see, the words in reported speech are very similar to the original ones used. There have, however, been some very important changes:

- a word has been added: **that**
- the verb *is* has changed to *was*   **tense change.**

When we write formal reported speech, we need to add the word *that*. If you want a more informal effect, you can omit *that*, but I suggest you keep using it until you are really familiar with writing reported speech.

We must also go back in time because we are now referring to something that happened earlier. We go back one **tense**. In the example above, the present simple tense has changed to the past simple. Look especially at the tense changes in the following examples:

Actual	The MPs said, "We won the battle for votes."	**Past simple**
Reported	The MPs said that they had won the battle for votes.	**Past perfect**
Actual	The MPs said, "We are winning the battle for votes."	**Present continuous**
Reported	The MPs said that they were winning the battle for votes.	**Past continuous**
Actual	The MPs said, "We were winning the battle for votes."	**Past continuous**
Reported	The MPs said that they had been winning the battle for votes.	**Past perfect continuous**

Don't feel that you need to learn the names of tenses. I've just put them in as a guide. Just focus on getting a *feel* for going back in time. When I learnt to teach English as a foreign language, I was taught to use lots of gestures. When I wanted students to use the past tense, I would jerk my thumb backwards over my shoulder. You might find it helpful to imagine doing this when you need to write reported speech. Visualizing what you need to do can be a very powerful reminder.

Before you get too confused over all this, it's a good idea to remember, as with many features of grammar, that you have almost certainly been getting it right, as you speak, for years.

The future tense can be a little tricky, but here again, you doubtless get it right when you speak. Here *will* changes to *would*:

Actual "We **will put forward** improved policies on housing and taxation," promised the members of the new party.

Reported The members of the new party promised that they **would put forward** improved policies on housing and taxation.

Concentrate on remembering that *will* changes to *would*. Technically speaking, the **future indicative** has changed to the **subjunctive mood**. But here we are touching on areas that are beyond the scope of this book.

Tenses and the word *that* are the key issues here, but there are also some other items that you will need to know about:

1 pronoun change
2 time change
3 place change
4 setting out questions
5 greetings.

You will find below a selection of examples for each of these items. Many of them are fairly obvious, but some are a little tricky.

1 Pronoun change

Actual "I'm finishing my essay," said Nick.

Reported Nick said that he was finishing his essay.

Actual "We went to the cinema," said the children.

Reported The children said that they had been to the cinema.

Actual Beverley said, "I'm exhausted."

Reported Beverley said that she was exhausted.

2 Time change

Actual "I bought a new car yesterday," said Ruth.

Reported Ruth said that she had bought a new car the day before.

> **Actual**   "I bought a new car <u>today</u>," said Ruth.
> **Reported** Ruth said that she had bought a new car <u>that day</u>.

> **Actual**   My sister said, "It's raining <u>now</u>."
> **Reported** My sister said that it was raining <u>then</u>.
>   or
>   My sister said that it was raining <u>at the time</u>.

3 Place change

> **Actual**   "I'm sure I put the money in <u>this</u> box," said Anne.
> **Reported** Anne said that she was sure she had put the money in <u>that</u> box.

> **Actual**   Rob said, "The letters are all <u>here</u>."
> **Reported** Rob said that the letters were all <u>there</u>.

4 Setting out questions

> **Actual**   "Where's the science block?" <u>said</u> John.
> **Reported** John <u>asked</u> where the science block was.
>   or
>   John <u>asked</u> for directions to the science block.

> **Actual**   "Why is Sam going?" <u>said</u> Ben.
> **Reported** Ben <u>asked</u> why Sam was going.

> **Actual**   "What's the time?" <u>said</u> Ben.
> **Reported** Ben <u>asked</u> what the time was.
>   or
>   Ben <u>asked</u> for the time.

Notice that in each of the above examples, the questioning word (*where, why, what*) is often repeated in reported speech, but that the order of words is different. Note also that we *never* use a question mark in reported questions. A reported question isn't asking anything; it merely shows that a question had been asked.

5 Greetings

> **Actual**   "Good morning, ladies and gentlemen," said Mr Fox.
> **Reported** Mr Fox greeted everyone.

ACTIVITY 3

See if you can now turn the following eight brief statements made by Mark into reported speech. The first one has been done for you.

1 "I drive to work every day," said Mark.
   Mark said that he drove to work every day.
2 "I am driving a Ford, now," said Mark.
3 "I drove to Italy last month," said Mark.
4 "I have driven 500 miles this week," said Mark.
5 "I have been driving for 10 years now," said Mark.
6 "I was driving at night when the brakes failed," said Mark.
7 "I will drive to Spain next year," said Mark.
8 "I will be driving a Porsche next year," said Mark.

SUMMARY

▶ Checklist for direct speech
- put speech marks around the *exact words spoken*
- begin with a *capital letter*
- keep punctuation *inside* speech marks
- use a lower case letter for *he said* and *she said*
- when following the speech with *he said/she said*, add a *comma* before closing the speech marks
- when using *he said/she said* before the words spoken, add a *comma* after *said*

▶ Checklist for reported speech
1 add the word *that*
2 go back one tense
3 check pronouns
4 check time and place

Part Two
Coping with Essays

6 Putting an Essay Together

I GETTING ORGANIZED

INTRODUCTION

If you are not in the habit of writing essays, you may be seriously concerned about having to begin. Writing your first essay is likely to be a time-consuming process, and many people become extremely worried about submitting this first effort. Sandra, one of my students, was afraid that I would think her work was childish. Another student, Bill, felt that if he didn't get everything right first time that there was no hope for him.

Neither student need have worried. Sandra needed to realize that everyone has something useful to say, even if at first they have difficulty expressing their ideas on paper, and Bill soon found out that we learn to write essays through practice. Your tutors are not likely to expect you to be able to submit competent essays without having learned how to do it.

If you are starting an A-level or an Access to Higher Education course, you are likely to find that things are rather different from what any of us did at school 10, 20, or more years ago. When we were given a title for an essay, we usually went away and wrote as much as we knew on the subject. Now, you are likely to be given a very specific question. This means that instead of writing all you know on a topic, you will need to select information that is relevant to that particular question.

Writing an essay is not like knowing the answer to a mental arithmetic sum. It's a *process*. It concerns time spent in gathering information, in working out what we think about various aspects of what we've studied, and in finding out how best to get the crucial issues on paper. Essays *grow*.

Different subjects have different ground rules. For example, if you are studying history, there will be great emphasis on evidence, on when this evidence originated, and on various accounts by later commentators of the period you are studying. In sociology, the emphasis is likely to be on theories about society and on surveys of different societies. If your subject is English literature, you will have found that you need to analyse language very closely, and pay attention to such things as plot and theme. If you are studying a science subject, you will be aware that you will need to focus on data, to show clear results, and to demonstrate how these are arrived at. It would be a good idea, therefore, before going any further, to jot down a list of what you know of the important criteria for your subject. This will get you thinking along the right lines.

Writing an essay is a very personal process. With a little practice, you will find your own ways of approaching the different parts of the work. Use this chapter to begin to find out what works for you, and feel free to adapt things to your own needs. You may find that, as you work, the stages I've outlined start to overlap or even change places. The crucial thing is that you submit a satisfactory assignment. How you get there is of little importance.

▶ Analysing the question

Why do essay questions look so difficult?
Sometimes, people are put off by the question itself. Essay questions often seem very complicated. Most of them turn out to be a lot less difficult than they at first appear, but if you are already feeling nervous, a difficult-sounding question can seem like the last straw.

Questions often look difficult because they are written in rather formal language. There are two possible reasons for this. The first is that the tutor has probably tried to be as precise as possible and to write something that cannot be misunderstood or read two ways. S/he is actually trying to be helpful. The other reason is that s/he will have set the question out in such a way as to put boundaries on what you do. If the topic is not restricted like this, you could end up doing much more work than is necessary. Oddly enough, it often turns out that questions which look easy prove to be harder to answer than those which appear more complex. A tightly-structured question will help to keep you on track.

Underlining the key words

Many people have learned the hard way that it is absolutely essential to *underline the key words* before you do anything else. If you get things wrong at this stage, all your work is likely to be wasted.

Never, ever, try to omit this stage. There are two reasons for this: you need to understand *exactly* what is wanted and you want to eliminate the possibility of making errors that would send you off in the wrong direction. It's so easy to misread a word or even to answer the question that you hoped you would be asked. That can sometimes happen when there's a topic that you're particularly interested in. The mind plays tricks, and you think you see the question that you want to answer, rather than the one that's actually been asked.

Let's suppose that you have been given the following essay question:

Discuss the proposition that education is wasted on the young.

You may have heard the saying 'Youth is wasted on the young'. This essay question derives from that statement and is deliberately controversial. It's not subject-specific, and was designed to enable mature students to use their knowledge of life and current affairs as well as giving them the opportunity to research an area of their choice.

I'll underline the key words:

<u>Discuss</u> the <u>proposition</u> that <u>education</u> is <u>wasted</u> on <u>the young</u>.

You'll find that, every time you do this, you will have underlined a large part of the question. You might wonder, then, why you need to bother. You might think, "Oh well, I'll just remember that I have to work on the whole thing." Well, do remember what I said above. There's another reason for underlining, however. What tends to happen when you underline is that your mind immediately begins to focus on what is going to need to be done. It begins to get into gear – even if you still feel you haven't got a clue on how to proceed.

Problem areas

It's also important to be clear on what is *not* asked. The question does not, for example, ask for a survey of current educational practice. So to do that would result in the award of a very low mark. Nor does it ask for a historical analysis or an analysis of practice in one school. Either of those two approaches would lead to an equally nasty grade.

The process of writing essays is a process of training the mind to think clearly. A good essay is one in which the student has stuck like glue to the key words in the question and so has done exactly what was asked. If, by any chance, you cannot make sense of the question, do go back to your tutor for help. Never try to begin a piece of work until you are quite clear on what's wanted.

You will very likely need to use a dictionary to make sure you are quite clear on the definitions of certain key words in the question. Be careful, however, over technical words that may have specific meanings for your subject. Technical words are not likely to be defined in a non-specialist dictionary, and you can easily be misled. For these you will need a dictionary that is subject-specific. This type of dictionary is available for most subject areas. On the other hand, the words you need may well appear on a handout you've been given or have been defined in a class session.

Never copy out definitions. Your tutor will not be impressed. What you may need to do, however, is to define exactly what *you* intend to mean by a particular word in the context of your essay. For words that have a number of meanings, it can be very important to isolate the one that you are dealing with.

Following the instructions

You'll have noticed that I also underlined the word *Discuss* in the essay question above. This is the instruction that tells you how to write up the material after you've got all your notes together.

You will often be asked to *discuss*. This means that you need to show both sides of a question – or more if more exist, and then to make your own judgement on which is/are the more useful. You do this after having taken account of the evidence. So your final judgement is likely to form the conclusion to your essay.

Instructions are vital. You could have been asked to *compare* the relative value of educating the young with that of educating mature students. That would mean that you would need to look specifically at results for each group and to give roughly equal space to a consideration of each. Clearly, an essay involving comparison would be very different from one involving discussion. So check carefully what you have been asked to do, and if you are not absolutely clear on what is required, do ask your tutor.

Here are some more **instructions** you might be given:

analyse:	examine in detail, showing pros and cons
assess:	weigh up the value of and give a judgement

compare:	show the similarities between two given items
contrast:	point out all the differences between items
criticize:	show both the good and bad points
define:	give the exact meaning of
describe:	give a detailed account of
explain:	make really clear, possibly giving examples and reasons
explore:	examine from various standpoints, showing the implications
outline:	give the main points of
summarise:	give a brief account of

Underlining the instructions as well as the rest of the question will highlight the way you need to approach the actual writing of the essay.

In the education essay, you have been asked to discuss a proposition. A **proposition** is just a statement for consideration. (In philosophy, it is a statement that may be either true or false.) In order to do this, you will need to isolate what seem to you to be the most important issues, to explain and comment on them and to draw a conclusion.

▶ Taking stock: making a mind map

The next stage is to construct a mind map. Don't worry, you are still allowed to be in a state of confusion. The whole point about all these activities is to get you going and keep you going – even though you may still feel that producing this essay is completely beyond you.

In this book, I have used the term *mind map* to refer to two different processes:

- getting ideas and inspiration
- making notes.

You may find the first of these referred to elsewhere as *brainstorming*. Either one can also be called making a spider diagram. Mind-mapping is a very useful technique which can also be used to take notes in lectures (see chapter 7) and to summarize topics for revision. A mind map is said to mimic the way our brains work, making connections that look more like a net than a straight line. So a mind map can be more useful than a list. Constructing a mind map is a way of setting out your ideas, or perhaps lack of them, in order to see what needs to be done next. The steps for this are:

1 write the question in capitals in the centre of a clean sheet of A4 paper
2 draw a box around the question
3 as each new idea comes to mind, draw a straight line from the box, and write the idea on this line in capitals, if possible in one word
4 add secondary ideas to individual ones as you think of them.

The important thing here is to put down all your ideas – the useful ones, the useless ones, and the totally crazy ones. The thing is to keep your thoughts moving and not to censor anything at all. Censoring can result in a blockage or in a drop in confidence. What you are after here is free flow, positive thinking, and confidence. Seemingly daft ideas can sometimes lead on to really good ones that have been lurking in your subconscious. So be as creative as you can.

You can see that, in the map I've drawn on the facing page, I managed to put my ideas down in three separate areas. This was really a matter of luck. You might find this a useful trick sometimes; but do whatever comes easiest. Generally speaking, it's always best to let your ideas come randomly.

A word here for tidy people: there are times when tidiness is highly valuable, but this is not one of them. Creativity won't occur when you are busy dotting i's, crossing t's and using a rubber. I'm very fond of a poem called 'The cast', by the Czech poet, Miroslav Holub, in which he talks about a magician:

> ... his cave is in such a mess that minor miracles occur
> spontaneously ...

Always give yourself space for *minor miracles* when you are doing any rough work.

When you have gone as far as you can with your map, you will have a good idea of what topics you are going to need to cover and also of what you are going to need to read up on.

▶ Doing your research

When you do background reading for an essay, you will be looking for evidence and examples that can be used to back up what you write. You'll be wanting to find out what key writers have said about your topic. It's probable that your tutor has given you a bibliography of the titles of useful books. In that case, stick to looking at things from this list. If you have no bibliography, ask your tutor to recommend something; if this fails, you'll always be able to find a friendly librarian who will help.

Don't, however, go home with a great pile of books. You won't have time to read them and the mere sight of the pile is likely to make you despair. You are not even going to read two books from cover to cover. Use **contents** and **indexes** to get straight to relevant sections. You'll be looking for facts and figures, ideas, and explanations of areas that have confused you. Facts and figures will be very important to you. These are the evidence you will use to prove the points you make in your essay. In many essays for humanities subjects, what you will be looking for are the ideas and views of various critics. Don't be fooled, however, into assuming that critics are always right. When you are sure of your ground, it's quite acceptable to challenge their ideas in your essays.

The section 'Note-taking from books' in Chapter 7 will explain how to go about using books. It's important to get plenty of notes together before you start to write. This will give you material to choose from and will also ensure that your essay has depth because your understanding of the topic area will be more developed. You may use only a small proportion of your notes, but you will have a good overview of the topic and you'll be able to choose just the most fitting items. (Whatever you don't use for your essay may well come in handy at exam time.)

▶ The plan: simple as ABC

When you have read up (and made notes on) the main areas you will be covering, it's time to make a plan of how you are going to construct your essay. This will give you a framework. Whatever the topic, your plan will fall into three sections:

Part A *introduction* (probably just one paragraph)
- indicate the main issues
- state what ground your essay will cover

Part B *middle*
- explain the issues and theories ⎫
- give examples and other evidence ⎬ comment as you go along
- show what others have said ⎭

Part C *conclusion* (probably no more than two paragraphs)
- sum up – referring to issues set out in the question
- state what you see as the most reasonable conclusion(s) to draw

Don't rush the planning stage. You need to do some careful thinking here. You will be marked on the structure as well as the content of your essays, so planning is very important. Go back to the title or question you've been given and take your cue from the key words. You'll find that your introduction and conclusion are likely, eventually, to take care of themselves (see below). The meat of your plan lies in the middle. So you need to decide what order you will use for the things you are going to cover.

Your plan will be a working document, however. If it turns out to be restrictive or unhelpful in any way, change it. Sometimes, students feel that there's no point making a plan in the first place if it's likely to be changed. It's only when you have created a structure, however, that you can begin to find out what does and doesn't work.

At this stage, you'll be likely to have a collection of some or all of the following:

- class notes
- handouts
- lecture notes
- notes from books, journals, etc.
- photocopies.

There is likely to be material you can use – even small items – in all of these. Most people find it helpful, when they've decided on the main structure of a plan, to colour-code the sections they want to use from their notes, handouts, and so on. This can save a lot of time because it means that you don't have to hunt for items when your mind is engaged on the writing process.

A good essay usually contains a clear line of **argument**. That doesn't mean that you need to get heated. It means that you need to think clearly about what you feel is the most valid interpretation of the issues you're covering and **comment** clearly on the material you cover.

By 'comment', I mean that you need to explain to the person reading your essay what you want him or her to *think* about the evidence you give. It is possible for two students to cite similar evidence and yet draw different conclusions from it. If you think for a minute about a court of law, you'll see what I mean: counsel for the prosecution and counsel for the defence will give completely different views of the evidence in their summing-up. What you as an individual make of the material is likely to be the key to getting good marks. Keep this in mind while you are making your plan. Aim to build up your points as you go along so that they will lead easily to your conclusion.

I've given below a simple plan that could be used for the education essay:

Discuss the proposition that education is wasted on the young.

I've focused on setting out the pros and cons for a discussion of the topic. If I am going to 'discuss' a statement, I must note points for and against and come to a balanced conclusion. Notice that I've built in a section for 'comment'. Each of your paragraphs will make a point, using some kind of evidence. You must comment clearly on the implications of that evidence. Note that if I were actually to write the essay I've planned below, my evidence would need to include figures, cite sources, and probably quote from my reading.

My plan shows just one way of structuring this essay. There are always many different ways to write a good assignment. What you do will depend on your own interests and experiences as well as on your individual way of working.

A: Introduction
Note that this is a v. broad statement – needs explanation
  Essay will: consider both sides of question re. value of education for young people & address issue of education for adults – especially contemporary courses

B: 1 – education is wasted on the young:
Main point: It could be argued that young people waste opportunities

Evidence	Comment
In late 20th-century Britain:	Look at possible causes:
violence in schools	violence at home, etc.
truancy rates up	disillusioned young – no hope of jobs
poor literacy levels	education not meeting needs

B: 2 – education is vital for the young:
Main point: There are many reasons why educating the young is essential.

Evidence	Comment
a child learns with ease –	essential to train sponge-brains of the
e.g. 2 languages at once	young

industrialized countries need many different types of workers	essential to train the workforce
children without education often turn to crime	society's moral duty is to educate the young – all societies have done it
children love to learn	a fulfilled child grows into a fulfilled adult

B: 3 – education for adults:

Main point: Since there are reasons why many children miss out on education, there are consequently many adults who want and need it. Note contemporary courses.

Evidence	Comment
adult students work v. hard	society has a moral duty to adults
Access courses etc. are booming	there is obviously a very wide need educating adults is cost-effective
society needs people to retrain for changing job market	

C: Conclusion

weight of evidence shows need for education at all ages because:
   value to any culture of educated citizens
   inescapable moral duty of the state to allow individuals to develop
      potential

From this plan, you could write a balanced essay that gives roughly equal weight to each of the three sections.

II: STARTING TO WRITE

INTRODUCTION

Many people find that the hardest part of writing an essay is actually getting started. Well, the good news is that you don't have to start at the beginning. You can, if you wish, start by working on the section that interests you most or that you find easiest. Your enthusiasm will then have a spin-off effect and you'll find it easier to do things you'd felt were more difficult. You may find it easier to use separate pages for different aspects of the topic. The main thing is to cover the ground – to get the whole thing on paper *somehow* without worrying much about grammar and punctuation. By the way, many people leave writing the introduction until last.

If you are really stuck, start by writing down something that your tutor – or another student – has said on the topic. You can always cross this out later. What you will be doing is tricking your mind into getting started. It doesn't matter what your first effort looks like. If you are hand-writing the essay, use one side of the paper only. You will see the importance of this when you come to redrafting.

By the way, don't fall into the trap of thinking that, because your tutor knows the subject inside out, you don't need to spell things out. The only way for him or her to find out whether *you* understand the topic fully is for you to get it on paper.

▶ Paragraphing

Knowing what to include in one paragraph or when to change to a new one are problems that worry lots of students. You have probably been told to start a new paragraph when you change to a new topic, but you may still not be too sure of where to make a break.

Planning your paragraphs

If you want to keep things really simple, it's possible to plan roughly the number of paragraphs you'll include before you even start to write. Look at the central part of your plan. Perhaps you've been asked to compare two particular issues or ideas. That would mean that you are likely to have a minimum of three paragraphs here: one for a description and explanation of each issue and one for the comparison. Perhaps you've been asked to explain a particular process and comment on it. That would mean you'll probably need one paragraph for each part of the process (assuming they are equally important), and one for the comment.

The middle section of your essay must have at least as many paragraphs as there are points in your plan. You may also need a paragraph for each crucial stage in your argument.

You'll see below a short piece written by Linda, a student starting out on a Sociology Access course. She was asked to read a couple of brief accounts by a man and a woman on how they each related to their local community. She then had to write 500 to 600 words on the question:

> *Why might men and women have different views on the existence of community?*

Read through Linda's essay and then look at my analysis of her paragraphs. I've numbered them to make things clear.

1   *Two people's views are shown, one male and one female. They are both quite different. The man states that when he was a child things were quite different, the streets were busy with chatting people, neighbours sat outside, and, he felt, there was generally a better community spirit than nowadays where he could walk down the street and not 'see a soul', and when he didn't know who lived 'two doors away'. On the other hand the female notes that a five-minute walk to the shops could take her up to three-quarters of an hour as she is often bumping into people she knows and chatting.*

2   *The difference in both of these views on the community is brought about by various differences in their lifestyles, and in society in general. Society has changed a great deal over the years and this is part of the reason why the male's view of community is so different to what it was in the past. Nowadays it wouldn't be safe to leave doors open, unlocked all through the day, or to leave chairs outside, in case of burglaries. Also as the standard of living increases in some areas, people move with a lot more freedom and frequency than they did years ago, which would account for his not knowing his neighbours. Also people's common interests change as moving occurs. Instead of most people living near each other working together, or in the same sort of places, like factories, mines, and other industries, as some of these have closed down and other jobs have taken over, men don't have that common link with each other that they did in days gone by.*

3   *Men also live and work and spend their leisure time in a different environment to women. Their 'space' is often a lot more restricted to their workplace, home, and often the pub. Obviously this is a generalization and some men have many other interests but they still don't move around the community and have as many*

'spaces' in the community as women. So often men don't know as much as women as to what goes on in their community.

4   Women's concept of the community is often entirely different. In the example, the woman obviously was involved in the community and knew a great many more people than the man did, which allowed her to make a five-minute shopping trip take three-quarters of an hour. Women who have children, even if they work, often spend a great deal more time in the community than men. Women have to be concerned, and get involved with, nurseries, schools, the shops, local activities for children, and many other things as well. At each of these places women meet different people, all with a common interest, children. If a woman is a mother then she has a connection with all the mothers in her area. When they meet, even as strangers in a doctor's or dentist's waiting room, they will have something in common which both will be knowledgeable about, their children.

5   This common interest breaks down a lot of barriers which may normally occur within a group in the community. Women are often more active in the community than men. It is usually the women who organize fund-raising events, set up self-help groups, protest over issues over housing, school cuts, nurseries, welfare issues, and other local services which may be under threat. This isn't because they have time on their hands, but rather because they are the ones more concerned with these issues, they have a clearer understanding on the effects these changes may cause to their community.

6   There are disadvantages for women who live in the community, in that it can confine and restrict them to living a very stereotypical life taken up with 'women's tasks', cooking, cleaning, and looking after children. Also if you're a woman who only has these chores in her life, with no outside community, such as someone living in a high-rise block of flats with no community spirit, then this life could become very lonely and isolated.

7   Women may also be constrained by not being financially independent and so having to rely on another's income could restrict socializing within their community. As well as this restriction on their leisure time, the fear of attack at night could also stop them socializing at night.

8   *So there are many reasons for the concept of community to be different for men and women.*

Linda's paragraphs split up her points like this:

Topic	Treatment
1 Introduction	Linda chooses key statements from what she's read to demonstrate differences between the man's and the woman's experiences of their local community.
2 New ways of living	Linda explains that these differences have been brought about by social and economic changes.
3 Men's lifestyles	Here she shows how daily life for a man may keep him apart from his local community.
4 Women's lifestyles	Now she shows how many of women's traditional concerns may have the opposite effect.
5 Women as activators in a community	Linda needed to begin a new paragraph here because, although this one is linked to the last by the 'common interest' of children, it deals with a new topic – the organization of self-help groups, protests, etc.
6 Disadvantages for women	This paragraph touches on possible negative issues resulting from women's community involvement. Linda is beginning to lose touch with the question here. It did not ask for anything on advantages or disadvantages.
7 Further disadvantages for women	This is really part of paragraph 6 because it just gives more examples of the same issue. Linda would have done better *not* to

begin a new paragraph here. She's also focusing heavily on women at the expense of men's experience.

8 Conclusion   This is rather brief. The conclusion needs to be a broader summing-up section.

It's a pretty safe bet that Linda's original plan for this piece of work looked very much like my list of numbered points. So I hope you can see from this how your plan and your paragraphs are likely to be very closely linked. This, however, was a very short essay. Obviously, things can get more complex with longer pieces of work.

How to construct a paragraph

A paragraph will always contain a key sentence. This is a sentence that sets out the main point in that paragraph. It is very often the first sentence, and, in order to make things easy on yourself, you might like to use that format with each of your own paragraphs.

The rest of the paragraph will elaborate on that key sentence. It is likely to contain explanation and comment – as in my paragraph above. It may also contain evidence and examples that will bear out what that key sentence states. If you look back at Linda's first paragraph, you will see that her key sentence comes first and that she then explains and expands on that sentence. Paragraphs 2, 3, 4 and 6 follow the same pattern. (You'll remember that I had reservations about her final two paragraphs.) In paragraph 5, the key sentence is the second.

Evidence, explanation and comment are the keys to a good essay. Every paragraph should contain one or more of these. You must also spell out any implications. Your tutor cannot be sure that you understand unless you make things quite clear. The fact that you were able to discuss the issue competently in a class session will not count. Marks can be given only for what you actually put on paper.

Linda's essay would have benefited from some reference to sociological theory. She's good, however, on giving examples and on explaining how they relate to her key statement. In paragraph 5, she gives a number of specific examples on women's community action and explains briefly how this comes about. Her first sentence sets the scene clearly by recalling what she had written in paragraph 4.

A paragraph could be said to be a bit like a mini-essay. It has an opening and a middle, and often an end which ties up this particular section. The reader needs to understand exactly what the writer feels about the relation of what he or she has stated to *the question itself*. You can do this very easily. You might use a sentence that starts like this:

> *It can clearly be seen from the above that ...*

The argument: linking one paragraph to the next

Clear linking is essential. Anyone reading an essay needs to be shown how one point leads to the next. This is partly to do with argument. You may remember that I mentioned argument in the section on constructing your plan. Your tutor needs to understand your particular angle on the material. Without links, he or she will have no clear idea of what you actually mean.

You may be feeling that you yourself haven't got much of a clue what you mean anyway. Well, that's not a serious problem because one of the functions of essay-writing is to force us to think and to clarify things in our own minds. We often don't know what we really think until we've tried to express it on paper. As you work on your assignment, you will almost certainly find that your ideas become clearer.

It's possible that you will have several consecutive paragraphs without links. You may be pretty sure that they fit together, but you can't quite see *how* to link them. Don't worry. Some form of linking is always possible. I'll demonstrate below how Linda coped with links in the education essay we've already been considering. It was given as an assignment on the core studies component of her Access course. I've numbered her paragraphs and added a résumé of each so that you can easily see the structure of the essay.

Discuss the Proposition that Education is Wasted on the Young

Introduction 1 *This essay will consider the proposition that education is wasted on the young. The basis for this discussion will revolve around formal education of four- to sixteen-year-olds.*

Points in favour of the proposition 2 *A reason why this proposition may be valid is the way in which attending school is enforced. For the age group mentioned above, all children are required to*

Enforced schooling can create problems	*attend school by law. This may induce some young people, of secondary school age especially, to rebel. This rebellion can be brought on by a number of factors. In secondary school mainly, young people come into contact with all sorts of influences as a whole new social scene emerges. These include drink, drugs, of which, previously, young people would have been sheltered from, at primary school. Pressures from their peer group, like keeping up with the latest fad, fashion, and pop sensations. Their appearance also becomes very important, as do relationships, both platonic and romantic. This is also the age when a romantic relationship may become more physical as the body undergoes great changes during puberty.*
Explanation of how the above may lead to waste	3 *Many young people who have a feeling of rebellion against the structure of school life, their teachers, the people in authority over them, would often be the ones to go down the road of drink, drugs, and this would often lead to truancy. Truancy would become a more and more common feature of their school life. This, in turn, would bring more pressure from parents and cause an aggravated home life. While young people are spending their time in this manner, you could say that their education is being wasted. The will to learn and be taught is overridden by the compulsion to defy.*
Adults given education use it to full advantage	4 *Another favourable factor in the argument that 'education is wasted on the young' is the growing demand for Adult Education. The large number of courses on offer to adults and the overwhelming success of these courses, shows how much more appreciated education is by the adult student. Also teachers on these courses do readily state how much more enjoyable it is to teach those willing to learn. Adults who come back into Education have the desire to learn a great deal more than the young. The big difference between adults learning and the young learning is the fact that it's the adult's choice. They actually want to be in the classroom, learning.*

**Points against
the
proposition**

**The majority
of teenagers
do not rebel**

5 *However, all of these previous arguments are not
conclusive. Teenage rebellion does not occur to such a
degree, as mentioned before, in every case. In the
majority of cases, this problem does not arise at all. A
lot of teenagers go to secondary school and have a
good rate of attendance. They don't play truant or get
involved with drugs or drink. They manage other pressures and their studies very well. In fact, peer groups,
and all they entail, benefit a lot of the young by teaching
them about social interaction. To use the pressures
teenager's face to prove that their education is wasted
is a gross generalisation. Not all young people give
in to these pressures by wasting their education. The
amount of colleges and universities greatly attended
across the country shows clearly just how many
youngsters make it through secondary school with
good grades. This showing how much education has
benefited them.*

**Most children
benefit from
education and
it can be a
vital antidote
to poverty**

6 *The argument against the structure and compulsory
nature of education also has its opposing side. A majority of children and teenagers benefit greatly from the
structure and compulsory nature of school attendance.
For many from a background of poverty, school can
mean a haven. A place which is warm and stimulating.
Also they have the benefit of a hot meal once a day.
This can be a contributing factor in a child's increased
learning capabilities.*

**More on
poverty**

**Value of
structure and
discipline**

7 *School can also mean an opportunity to escape from
a way of life which a child is born into. Without education a child born into a situation of poverty would be
less likely to have the ability to improve his, or her,
future life. Education gives any child the basis to
improve their employment prospects. Another way
which can aid in a child's future is the actual structure
and discipline of formal Education. This is extremely
beneficial, if, from a child's home life little or no discipline is given. The young need guidelines to be able to
live and grow so that they can function in society.*

School can
educate for
jobs/life

8 *Another beneficial aspect of formal education is the type of education that children are being taught. The technology taught in school, such as computers, equips them to be able to deal with such things in the outside world. In this age this knowledge is essential. As is the education given about sexual behaviour and the effects of drink, drugs, and smoking. A lot of children need this type of education as they might not receive any such knowledge at home.*

Great value of
primary
schooling

9 *An overwhelming fact contrary to the proposition, is the amount which children learn in Primary Schools. This early stage of a child's education is, in the vast majority of cases, very well received. The amount of information absorbed by primary age children is staggering. To watch, through education, a child of four, begin school, and within a matter of weeks be able to read their first books, is astonishing. To witness education being enjoyed by children first hand, immediately gives the proposition that education is wasted on the young a major flaw.*

Conclusion

10 *To conclude this discussion, the 'proposition that education is wasted on the young' from the arguments given, would be to say that the proposition is such a generalisation that it cannot be accurate. It could be found that some education is wasted on some young people, but even to prove even this would need a lot more research.*

Linda's overall structure is simple: points in favour of the proposition followed by points against. Let's look, first of all, at how she has achieved links between paragraphs:

PARAGRAPH 2
Linda's first sentence here uses the word *this*, which is a really useful word for first sentences. When added to an item from the previous paragraph – *this proposition* – it makes an immediate link.

PARAGRAPH 3
Here the link is more subtle. In paragraph 2, Linda spoke of *some young people*. Now she refers to *Many young people*. So the reader is kept

aware that this paragraph will continue to look at the topic already raised.

PARAGRAPH 4
The use of the word *Another* is a very straightforward way to make a link. Linda has followed it immediately with a reference to what she's talking about at this point – that is, *beneficial aspects of formal education*. The reader is being kept informed of exactly what the writer means.

PARAGRAPH 5
The word *however*** is especially handy. It signals a change of direction. What follows will be in some way different to what has gone before.

PARAGRAPH 6
The link is not quite so strong here, but Linda does refer helpfully to a previous point in the essay in her first sentence.

PARAGRAPH 7
The word *also* shows that the next point has a close relation to the last.

PARAGRAPH 8
Here is another subtle link. Linda has used that simple word *Another* and added it to a phrase – *beneficial aspect of formal education* – that functions as a reminder of the fact that she's now looking at points against the proposition.

PARAGRAPH 9
The phrase *An overwhelming fact contrary to the proposition* builds neatly on what has gone before.

PARAGRAPH 10
The general drift of this is clear, although the structure and phrasing are a little weak. It's not a good idea to tell the reader that you are now writing your conclusion: that's obvious. Linda refers here to the material she's covered in her essay with the words *from the arguments given*.

If you now look back over this analysis, you will find that, as well as

---

* *For students whose main subject is English*: It's better not to put the word *however* at the beginning of a sentence. Here, it could go at the end. Often it fits best in the middle, as in 'All the previous arguments, however, are inconclusive.'

making for smooth reading, Linda's links perform two other crucial functions: they help to set out her argument and they demonstrate its relation to the essay question itself. Throughout your essay, *everything* you write must relate to the question and you must *spell out* this relation. Good links are vital for this process.

More words and phrases which can be used for linking:
in addition to this
besides
despite this
in contrast to this
therefore
the above shows that
although
similarly
notwithstanding that
as a result
moreover
it follows from this that

You will also have noticed that Linda restricts the range of her discussion to four- to sixteen-year-olds. It's perfectly reasonable to put boundaries on your discussion. You can't cover everything. Of course, you will need to make sure that you don't omit anything vital; but, generally speaking, as long as you make it quite clear what you intend to cover, there should be no problem. It's often a good idea to check out your intentions with your tutor before you start. Requirements are likely to vary.

Paragraphs that are too long
Like punctuation, paragraphing helps the reader to understand your meaning. It sorts a piece of writing into sections and breaks it up into manageable chunks. If there's too much going on in one paragraph, a reader may start to get bogged down. So if you have a handwritten paragraph that is a page or more long, check to see whether it contains more than one issue.

Paragraphs that are too short
If a paragraph covers only two or three lines or is composed of only one or two sentences, it's almost certainly too short. There are two

possibilities here: it may fit better as part of the preceding or the following paragraph, or it may need expansion. I'd lay bets that it needs expansion. You've almost certainly raised a new idea that now needs explanation, examples and comment. The fact that you've written very little on it may indicate that you know less about this than other issues covered in you essay. It's no good, however, raising an issue and then leaving it hanging in mid-air. Either cut this paragraph out altogether or add sufficient data and comment.

Paragraphing complex topics

Paragraphing is usually fairly straightforward at points where you are moving from one clearly defined issue to another. The difficulty comes when you are dealing with a number of issues related to one topic. Boundaries can then get blurred and it's much more difficult to know where to make the breaks. Have a look at the following paragraph from an undergraduate essay on subjective views of class structure. It would be much better split into two paragraphs. Where would you make the break?

> The authors [of a particular survey] *state that aspirations for status-raising through friends was negligible – friends who had interesting work, a good education or 'a bit of class'. Considering the wording of that last phrase, it is surprising that anyone admitted to agreeing with it. There is a case here for using methodology from psychology to structure questions and interpret replies. It is likely that people who choose friends according to their social standing are unaware of what they are doing, and would therefore not agree that they chose people who had 'a bit of class about them'. The specific questions on residence and occupation would probably yield data on whether or not a respondent associated with people from a different social background. However, the question of why they had associated with them would still be unanswered. The terminology itself is restricting and provides added restraint on answers over and above the highly structured nature of the interviews. The section on residence shows the same problems. For those who wanted to move house, respectability of area was said to be more important than somewhere 'select'. In each case, respondents were asked for one answer, unlike Hillier's* [another sociologist] *method of taking into account secondary conceptions. For the Luton sample, who were highly geographically mobile, and therefore lacked the support of kin, respectability might be quite likely to be their first priority. However, further data and analysis may well have shown up other (and possibly equal) priorities, particularly if respondents had been encouraged to formulate their own responses.*

I'd break this paragraph after 'structured nature of the interviews'. That last sentence would form a good conclusion to the paragraph. The phrase 'the same problems' in what would be the first sentence of the new paragraph then forms a good link to what has gone before. Breaking up the material like this makes it much easier on the reader.

▶ Language and clarity

When you write your final draft, you'll need to be sure not to write just as your thoughts flow. It's essential to move from thinking to writing clear, grammatical sentences.

You might like to think back to my explanation of why we punctuate. Good essays are those which make the writer's ideas really clear to the reader – that is, your tutor. It makes no difference that your tutor may have been teaching for 30 years: he or she needs to be helped to understand *exactly* what *you* are getting at.

You don't need to try to sound like a textbook; write in a simple and straightforward manner. It's a good idea to aim to write in such a way that your work could be understood by an intelligent reader from a *different* subject specialism. This means that you'll use technical terms only when strictly necessary, that you'll explain your ideas fully, and that you'll be as precise as possible.

Academic writing is logical and unemotional, factual and precise. Because of the need for precision, we have to be especially careful not to state that something is the case if there is the least chance that it might not be so. A good way of getting around this sometimes is to say things such as:

It is *likely* that x is the case

or

x *seems* to be the case

Saying things in this way allows you to show both that you know the possibilities and that you are aware of the pitfalls. Don't overdo this trick, however. You don't want your tutor to complain that you always sit on the fence.

There are a few things that constantly cause people trouble. It's important to remember each of the following:

- *write impersonally* (i.e. without using the word 'I')
- *omit clichés* and slang expressions
- find the *exact word* for what you want to say
- keep to the *same tense* throughout
- write *all words in full* (i.e. don't abbreviate).

Writing impersonally

Nowadays, some tutors are happy to accept essays containing the word *I*, but your work will be more sophisticated if you learn to write impersonally. Some people feel that they *must* write in the first person. "If I've written the essay," they say, "I must admit that the views in it are mine." The simple answer to this is that if an essay has your name on it, it is very clear that the views in it are yours. Don't worry about sounding pompous and authoritative. Your tutors are looking for essays that show strength of purpose.

An essay that does not contain the word *I* actually comes across much more forcefully. The statement

Education for adults is essential.

seems somehow to have more validity than the statement

I think education for adults is essential.

The words *I think* introduce an element of doubt. They imply that maybe other people think differently. The first statement is adamant, although it contains no obvious emotion.

Clichés

Clichés can be a problem for new writers because we all start by expressing what we want to say in the words we've picked up from TV, newspapers, and whatever else we've read. Clichés are over-used, worn-out phrases that have lost their bite – such as *in this day and age*, *tried and tested*, *the bottom line*, and so on. Wherever you can, say things clearly in your own way. I've almost certainly used a few clichés in this book, but I'm not writing a strictly academic work. Since I want to chat to you, a few clichés are bound to creep in. It's especially important to avoid *slang*, however, as this can spoil the texture of your work and even make it look as though you are not thinking clearly.

Using the right word

Finding the right word for what you want to say can also be a bit time-consuming, but it's rewarding to be able to express exactly what you mean rather than approximately. A thesaurus may help you here, but often it's a case of learning as you go along, as sometimes you will just be unaware of definitions. Note very carefully which words your tutor has marked on your work, and aim to get on close terms with your dictionary.

In this example from an essay on Shakespeare's *Hamlet*, Christine, an A-level student, is clearly trying to sound formal:

> *Hamlet shows his love for Ophelia on many occasions and it appears more obvious than the ways in which Ophelia's love towards Hamlet is discerned.*

The word *discerned* – that is, perceived – must relate to the responses of the audience. It is they who perceive what is going on. But that sentence focuses on the behaviour of the two characters. It can't easily change focus to the behaviour of the audience. Maybe Christine actually meant *displayed*, which would fit much better. Perhaps the problem came about because she didn't want to use the word *shown* as she'd already used *shows*, and she got a bit confused. You can often spot this kind of thing when you are redrafting your work (see below).

Tense

Changing **tense** by mistake is another common problem. You will find out whether you've done this if you look for it specifically when you proofread (see below). It's a particular issue for those who are studying literature. When talking about a character in a book, it's fatally easy, for example, to swap back and forwards between *he did* and *he does* without realizing what we are doing. At the beginning of an essay, decide which tense you want to use and stick to it.

Abbreviations

Generally speaking, abbreviations should not be used in essays. Things like *i.e.* and *e.g.* are not admissible. You may, however, be given some assignments in which particular abbreviations are acceptable, especially in science or technology. Check with your tutor.

Raising questions

Some people feel that formulating questions can be a useful means of drawing attention to particular arguments. When giving a talk, this is fine, but in written work, it can end up by being more trouble than it's worth. Assuming you've remembered to use the question mark itself (see chapter 3), there are further problems to negotiate.

If you are a student, you are likely to find that your tutor is not too keen on you putting questions in your essays – especially if you are a humanities student. The reason for this is that asking questions rather than making statements can give the impression that you don't really know what you are talking about. But that's not all.

Generally speaking, when you are writing an essay you are already grappling with a question you've been given. That's usually a hard task in itself. Raising more questions can just make the whole thing more complicated because once you've asked a question yourself, you really need to try to answer it – or, as I said, you can appear to be less than clued-up.

Technically speaking, this approach can get you into a real minefield because of difficulties with grammar and construction, both of individual sentences and of the essay itself. I've known students tie themselves in knots trying to answer extra questions that they've raised themselves while still struggling to answer the main essay question set by their tutor.

Sometimes, however, you will need to talk about questions that other people have raised about various issues, and it's important that you set these out really clearly. For this, you need to understand *the difference between the question itself and a statement of this question.*

Let's assume that you have been asked to write a report on a class discussion on the subject of poverty in the Third World, and that during the discussion, one student, Tom Rush, said, "How can governments co-ordinate a global approach?"

When you write your report, you *could* merely repeat Tom's question:

> *One student said, "How can governments co-ordinate a global approach?"*

But that may look a little simplistic. A better way of doing it would be to *report* what Tom said. (See the section on reported speech in chapter 5.) This means that you will rephrase the question so that it becomes a statement – like this:

> *One student raised the question of how governments would be able to co-ordinate a global approach.*

Notice that when I've used the student's *actual words*, I've added a question mark, but that when I've *reported* his question, I've used only a full stop. This is very important. A question mark should be used *only* after a question.

One thing you want to avoid at all costs is *combining* a question with a statement.

I've seen people treat an item like the one above something like this:

> One student said how governments would be able to co-ordinate a global approach to the problem of Third World poverty?

Either use the exact question (with its question mark) *or* report it (without a question mark).

Now you may be feeling that it is essential to mention questions that frequently come up in relation to certain topics. You may want to show that you are aware of these. Or you may want to show that a particular view is not foolproof and that questions *should* be asked about it.

I suggest that you cope with this in a similar way to the way in which I reported on Tom Rush's question. Suppose you are writing an essay on the current state of secondary education in Britain. You have mentioned the relevant Acts of Parliament and various other government initiatives, and you have looked at classroom practice. Now you want to conclude your essay by asking the following questions:

1 Why isn't more money spent on education?
2 Why are parents not expected to be more involved in schools?
3 Why doesn't Britain try to learn more from European education systems?

You need to turn those questions into statements – like this:

> *The most useful measure that government could take to improve education in our secondary schools would be to spend more money. If parents were routinely involved much more closely in their children's education, the public would become far more aware of the cost of good systems and would accept the inevitable increase in taxes. Finally, it is clear that Britain could learn a good deal on structuring an education system from its near neighbours, France and Germany.*

That simple process has transformed the questions into a forceful conclusion.

▶ Drafting and redrafting

Occasionally, at the beginning of a course, tutors will ask you to submit both an essay itself *and* your plan and rough drafts. What they'll be looking for is evidence that you have moved through a *process* – beginning with ideas that may well be vague and a draft that is probably messy and even rather incoherent – to a finished product which is clear and neatly organized.

This is the process through which any serious writer will go. No published book or article arrives on the author's desk fully formed. Everybody adds things, deletes, makes changes, and puts whole sections in the bin. This particular chapter, for example, has been moved from a different part of the book, been completely reorganized, and had scores of additions and alterations.

If you handwrite, it's a good idea to leave a line between paragraphs. It makes your work look really neat, enables anyone reading it to see clearly where paragraphs start and end, and gives tutors space to add comments. So I'd suggest you write this way from the start – even in your first drafts. You are likely to find that the extra space is handy for additions while you are redrafting.

Some people like to write a first draft really quickly, getting all their ideas on paper before settling down to look more carefully at various items. Others work best in a slower, more reflective manner, thinking things through as they go along. You will soon find what works best for you.

When you have completed the first draft, it's a good idea to leave it on one side for a day or two if you have time. Then when you return to it, you will look at it with a fresh eye. First of all, you'll need to look at structure. You want to check that the points you've made follow clearly from one another, and that anyone reading the essay would find it easy to follow. Then check for sufficient factual material and comment.

An analysis similar to the one a carried out above on Linda's work on male and female views of a community can be a very valuable exercise to perform on one of your own essays. By looking really closely at what you've written and jotting down a note of what's going on in each paragraph, you can get an overview of the essay and you'll be able to see clearly if there's anything wrong with the structure.

So you may find that you need to reorder things. Life will be a lot easier now if you have used only one side of the paper. Why? Because you can take a pair of scissors, cut the thing up, and stick it together in a revised order.This will give you a feeling of control over your work as you take charge of the editing process.

If you have used a computer, of course, you can move sections around with ease. I'd suggest, however, that you work from a printout rather than trying to do the whole job on screen. Most people find that it's easier to see what needs to be done if they can have the complete piece of work in front of them.

If you have access to a computer but are new to using it, do get someone to show you how to save your drafts on disk. It can be agonizing to lose work that you've spent hours – or even days – over. Keep your printouts, too, until you've submitted the final draft.

My own method is to write the first draft in pencil. When I have this complete, I get it on the computer. When I have my first printout, I can begin to see the wood for the trees, so to speak. From here on, I make alterations on the printout (often in red, so that I can spot them easily) until it's starting to get messy, and then I go back to put these on the computer. Then I do a second printout. This process goes on until either I'm happy with the result or I've run out of time. Some people manage to do alterations straight on to the computer. I do this for simple changes, but I prefer to sit quietly to think about more complex issues.

When redrafting, keep an eye out for anything that doesn't specifically answer the question – such as background information on a novelist or scientist, or details of another topic that you happen to be good at. Unrelated information is actually likely to lose you marks. You need to develop a sniffer-dog's nose for the right material.

Redrafting does not necessarily mean wholesale change, however. It also covers attending to all the items listed in 'Proofreading', below.

▶ Proofreading

Your final draft needs to be checked for spellings, grammatical problems, and other minor errors. It's often easiest to do a separate read-through for each type of error so that you can concentrate on one at a time. As your course progresses, keep a note of tutors' comments on your work and of the errors that you've made. You are very likely to find that you keep making similar mistakes. This is quite usual, but it will go on happening until you address the issues consciously. So make yourself a list on a piece of card and have it by you when you are proof-reading. This way you'll progress really fast. (See the Appendix for spelling strategies.)

You will want your work to read smoothly. You may find that you have some long, unwieldy sentences that don't seem to say quite what you mean. You might sort this out by splitting the sentences up into shorter ones. Each sentence might cover one small stage in a process or one step in an argument. (Chapter 8 will help you with complex sentences.)

So when you proofread, ask yourself the following questions:

- Are grammar and spellings accurate?
- Have I made any of my usual errors?
- Does the essay read smoothly?
- Does it make sense? Have I said what I mean?

If you can put yourself in the reader's shoes, you will be more able to pick up problems of sense and logic.

▶ Learning from feedback

Tutors spend hours marking essays. The comments they write on your work are specific to you and designed to help you to progress. You will often find that they have added factual items and useful analysis. If you can't follow what's been said on your work, do see your tutor and ask for more explanation. Understanding what has been written can be crucial for your next assignment. Tutors are always pleased to find that a student is making good use of comments on an essay.

If there are an awful lot of corrections on your work or if you've got a bad grade, even though you've worked hard, try not to despair. It really is all part of the learning process. I once nearly gave up all my studies quite early on over a bad grade. I'm very glad I didn't. There are gurus in the business world who state categorically that if you are not making mistakes you are not getting anywhere. They are far happier to see employees working creatively and getting some things wrong than playing safe and never opening up new horizons.

SUMMARY

▶ The four steps for getting organized

- analyse the question: key words and instructions
- make a mind map of what you know and/or need to find out
- do some research and take notes
- draw up a plan

▶ Issues to keep in mind when writing and submitting essays

- the question
- your argument
- paragraphing
- linking
- clarity and language
- how to raise questions
- drafting and redrafting
- proofreading
- feedback from tutors

7 Taking Notes and Using Quotes

INTRODUCTION

If you haven't done any studying for years, it's likely that you may be worried about note-taking. When you haven't had much practice of doing this, it's hard to know what you need to write down. There are two main types of note-taking: recording the important points from a lecture or class session, and making notes from your reading. The reason for making notes, of course, is to help you with:

- assignments
- exams.

So this is a crucial part of your course.

There are various ways you can make notes, and what you do will depend partly on the subject you are studying and partly on your own personal preferences. After looking at ways of recording key points from lectures and class sessions, and of taking notes from books, this chapter will cover all you need to know about supplying the necessary records of your reading and quotations. If you are studying English, you will find that the section 'Quoting from literature' will be especially useful.

▶ Note-taking in lectures and class sessions

As soon as you start attending a course, you will need to make notes, and the first problem is likely to be knowing how much to write down. You will probably find that some of the other students end up with writer's cramp because they write all the time, and some seem to sit through a whole session and write down practically nothing.

Neither of these methods is likely to be much help to you in the long run. In any class or lecture session, you need to spend some time considering what's being said, so if you spend all your time writing, you will have missed out on mulling over ideas as they come up and on taking part in discussions. If, on the other hand, you write down very little, you will have to rely heavily on your memory, and few of us have memories capable of retaining a lot of new facts and ideas in one go.

What you need are notes that give you a lot of information in a very readable format. Notes written in sentences are not going to make things easy for you. They not only take too long to write, but they take too long to read as well.

It makes sense, therefore, to develop a method that's going to be of most use to you. It may take a little practice to change your habits, but it's well worth the effort. You just haven't time to write everything in full if you're going to cope with a demanding course.

Watch for the way a class session or lecture is structured. Some tutors start with an introduction in which they tell you what will be covered; so if you know there will be three sections, mark them out as you go along. This will help you to feel in control of the situation. Your **syllabus** may have given you some clue as to which are the important areas to concentrate on, so listen out for those when you attend a lecture. You may be given a handout that shows the key areas of the day's topic. Use this as a guide. There may even be spaces for you to fill things in as you go along.

Quite often, the way a person speaks can give a clue to important points: a tutor's voice may rise, she may stress certain words very strongly, or she may pause before an important point or even repeat a phrase or two. Listen out for what seem to be key words and ideas. Underline, ring or highlight these. Sometimes there will be examples or an explanation that you can jot down briefly. It is possible to use your page rather like a drawing board, ignoring the printed lines if that's easier. Don't worry what your notes look like. All that matters is that they are useful for you.

Here are some tips for surviving a lecture:

- check your syllabus beforehand to see how this lecture fits in
- note key headlines on any handouts provided
- pay special attention to the introduction
- listen for words or phrases that are stressed
- write down three questions before the lecture starts.

Devising specific questions before going into a lecture can help to focus your mind on what's to come. Just spending a few minutes thinking about the topic will help to get your brain in gear.

Below is an extract from Mick's notes from a lecture on Marx and Engels' views on religion. He has adapted the mind-mapping technique shown in chapter 6 on essays. Here he's moving from the top of the page downwards in the way Westerners generally write. He's used rings, boxes, underlinings and capitals to make things stand out. For example, the word *alienation* is boxed because it's a key idea in Marxist thinking. Mick's notes have been reduced in size.

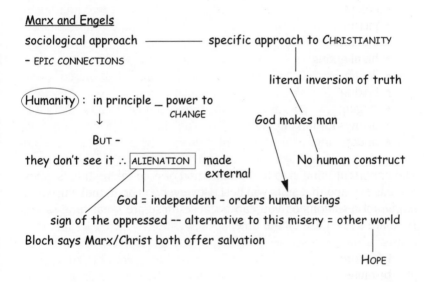

The main things to notice here are:

- only a few key words are written down
- lines are drawn to link points
- there's space to add things later.

There will always be things you miss. But if you read over your notes on the same day as your lecture, you are likely to be able to remember and fill in extra points while your memory is still fresh. This is one of the best ways of helping to make the material stick in your mind. If you can make time for a brief study session with a friend, between you you'll probably get all the important points down.

Always leave plenty of space on each page so that you can fill things in afterwards. Weeks later – or when you are revising – you may come across something you need to add. It's infuriating if there's no space. Not only that – a cramped page can be a frightening prospect when you come to revise.

When going over your notes, you can add colour-coding for different topics or processes. All of the following are great for helping things stick in your mind:

- mind maps
- patterns
- colour
- pictures
- diagrams
- highlighting
- listing
- boxing
- ringing
- arrows for linking
- underlining.

The important thing is to find the method of note-taking that is quickest, easiest, and that suits you best. However you do it, make use of as many abbreviations as you can because these are great time-savers. Here are a few I use all the time:

therefore	∴
because	∵
is	=
isn't	≠
twentieth century	㉉
nineteenth century	⑲
more than	>
less than	<

Get into the habit of making your own short forms for words you use often. Here are some of mine:

history	hist.
literature	lit.

| psychology/psychological | psych. |
| tradition | trad. |

Taking notes can be quite hard work, and you'll probably find it easier if you adopt a good posture. I've also noticed that if, for example, I'm listening out for budget tax changes on the radio, I have little trouble in hearing exactly what I need to know because I'm so alert. The more you are interested in your subject, the easier it will be to spot crucial points in what you hear.

If you need to get in some practice in note-taking before starting a course, and you are able to be in the right place at the right time, you might try listening to some Open University programmes. These are designed to be especially helpful for note-taking and are very well structured. Go for radio rather than TV programmes so that you won't be distracted by a picture. You are sure to be able to find a programme that relates to your own subject.

▶ Note-taking from books

In all forms of note-taking, key words and sentences are what you're after. Note-taking from books can be the best way to practise this. You won't have the advantage of hearing someone stressing the main points (and perhaps being able to ask them questions), but you can watch for headings and words in bold or italic type, and you can, of course, work at your own pace.

Here, you will be guided by the task or assignment you've been set. You're almost certainly going to be either writing an essay or preparing to give a short talk or a seminar paper. It's a good idea to have a note of the task in front of you so that you focus your reading clearly on the required area and so prevent yourself from wasting time on things that aren't relevant. *Never* spend time on books that you find dull or that are only vaguely related to your subject; and never make notes on even a whole chapter unless it is brim-full of ideas and data that are relevant to your assignment. Pick and choose just the things you need.

We all develop our own methods of note-making. There are, however, several things you will need to do. Always take a fresh sheet of paper and write at the top:

- the title of the book
- the full name of the author
- the publisher
- the date and place of publication.

Many of us learn this the hard way, finding that we have scraps of paper containing disconnected notes and no reference to where they came from. You can't use ideas or quotations in your assignments without saying where you got them from. So without a name and title, your work is wasted.

One of the most important things when note-taking from books is to *differentiate between your own words and those of the author*. If you want to make a note of an idea or an explanation, you will need to put it in your own words. Doing this is good practice, as it will help you to understand the idea more clearly and remember it more easily. On the other hand, you may feel that the author has said something so well that you would like to quote his or her exact words. This has to be done very carefully. I'll explain by showing you some of my own notes (see below).

When I was studying sociology, my course included a section on the structure of modern families, and the set book was *The Family and Marriage in Britain* by Ronald Fletcher, first published in 1962. I had to write an essay with the title:

> *Critically discuss Fletcher's account of the genesis of the modern family and its workings.*

So I needed to find out from the book not just specific facts and figures but, particularly, Fletcher's own views on the topic. The book is written very clearly, so it was not too difficult for me to make my notes. Here is the beginning of them:

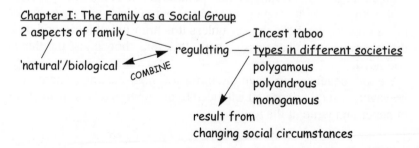

2 conceptions of marriage

Barbara Wootton ——————— religious
                            utilitarian (p. 40)

P40   Marriage exists to found & maintain the family
P41   'involuntary' grouping for children
41/2 Great intimacy – long period – determines psychological health
       etc. of its members
43   ' "educative" group of the most fundamental kind' for children.
       Family = primary group – general society comprises secondary
       groups.
45   Family background influences all future behaviour. Each member
       brings ideas etc. from outside that react on others.
46   Try for balance – inside/outside – espec. for child.

You can see that at first I decided to try using the method of note-taking that I used in lectures. This is really clear and handy for revision. But as I read on, two things were happening. I was finding it harder to fit complex ideas quickly into an easy-to-read format, and I was occasionally wanting to quote some of the writer's exact words. You can also see that I suddenly started to use page numbers all the time. I obviously realized that I might need these.

Page numbers are essential for:

(a) showing exactly where you found material that you quote
(b) finding your way back to a point you want to check.

If I show you a short section from *The Family and Marriage in Britain* (pp. 42–3), you can see that I tried to pull out key points and to avoid making notes on sections that just *elaborate* on these:

> Hence the family is that group within which the most fundamental appreciation of human qualities and values takes place – 'for better for worse': the qualities of truth and honesty, of falsehood and deceit; of kindliness and sympathy, of indifference and cruelty; of cooperation and forbearance, of egotism and antagonism; of tolerance, justice and impartiality, of bias, dogmatism, and obstinacy; of generous concern for the freedom and fulfilment of others, of the mean desire to dominate – whether in

overt bullying or in psychologically more subtle ways. All those values, and all those discriminations and assessments of value, which are of the most fundamental importance for the formation of adult character are first experienced and exercised by children in the context of the family. Furthermore, these qualities are not 'taught' or 'learned' in any straightforward or altogether rational way; they are actually embodied in people and their behaviour. The child perceives them and appraises them in concrete and demanding situations, and in direct face-to-face relationships with people who matter supremely. In this way, the family is an 'educative' group of the most fundamental kind.   *

My only note for this whole section is to jot down part of Fletcher's key sentence. I've ignored all the explanatory examples.

▶ **Quoting**

This section will cover setting out your quotations. In the section 'References and bibliography' you will find an explanation of how to record page numbers and other details.

The basic thing to remember is that when you quote from a book, you can copy a whole sentence (sometimes more) or just a word or two. You can see that on page 41 of Fletcher's book, I found a single word that I wanted to quote. This is Fletcher's whole sentence:

> It should be noted, that, for the children especially (but, to varying degrees, for the parents too), the family is an involuntary grouping.   *

I might have expressed this in my own words by saying that a child can't choose its parents, but I don't think I'd have thought of using the word *involuntary*. It puts the idea very neatly into formal terminology, so it's essential that I give Fletcher the credit for it. I've done this by putting quotation marks round it.

As it happened, I did not, eventually, use this in my essay. You may use only a small proportion of the notes (and quotes) you make from your reading. But that's fine. The idea is to be well prepared; then, when you are writing an essay, you will have plenty of material to choose from and your work will not lack depth.

My quote from Fletcher's key sentence on page 43 concerns the way in which children learn behaviour from family members. The first thing to notice here is that Fletcher himself has put a word in quotation marks. Occasionally, we use these marks to signal that the word inside them is not being used in the usual or strictest sense. Here Fletcher is making it quite clear that, within families, children are not taught or educated in the way that teaching goes on in schools.

I had to be very careful to keep Fletcher's own quotation marks in place. This meant that I had to use *two sets* of marks: one set for the word he himself had put in quotation marks and another set to enclose the whole of the section I was quoting. If I had then wanted to use that statement in my essay, I might have done it like this, putting double quotation marks around *educative* in order to make a distinction between this and the single marks I've used for the whole quotation:

> *Fletcher stresses that, for children, a family is an '"educative" group of the most fundamental kind.'*

It's quite acceptable to start and stop a quote whenever you like in order to suit the purpose of your own writing. Although you must show any punctuation that appears *within* the quote, you may terminate your quote *before* a punctuation mark if it makes sense to do that. If I wanted to show how Fletcher describes the way in which children pick up behaviour from those around them, I could do this without having to incorporate his full stop after 'behaviour':

> *Fletcher shows how children absorb 'qualities' that 'are actually embodied in people and their behaviour' through daily contact with members of the family.*

By the way, although the lines or single words that you copy from a book are called a **quote,** they only turn into a quote when you have copied them – or when you repeat them aloud to someone else. In their printed form in the text, they are not a quote. People sometimes get confused over this.

Indenting

You may have noticed that I didn't use quotation marks for the extracts from *The Family and Marriage in Britain* that are printed above (marked with an asterisk). The reason for this is that I've **indented** them. That is, I've used a wider margin than usual on each side of the page. I've also left a line before and after each quote. If you want to quote more than just a few words, set the quote out like that and it will show up clearly on your own page.

Be careful not to overdo quotes, however, or you are likely to be accused of padding or of failing to explain things in your own words. Your tutors want to be sure that you have understood what you have read, and to do this they need to see your own explanations. It's almost impossible to generalize, but a reasonable rule of thumb is not to have more than two quotes for each page you hand-write, and, in general, not to quote more than two or three lines at a time.

The problem of the half-way house
It's very important to make a clear difference between putting something in your own words and quoting directly from what you've read. Sometimes, students get muddled and seem to try to do both at once, and this can make an essay confusing and difficult to read. The following sentence suffers from this problem:

> 'Fletcher says the child perceives qualities and appraises them in the family and is educated in this way.'

Quotation marks must be used for *the exact words as written in the text* you are using. They are *never* used for approximations or for your own explanation. Give the name of the writer, and explain what he or she wrote, using quotation marks solely for the exact words that you lift from the text. Sorted out, that sentence above might become:

> Fletcher states that a 'child perceives ... and appraises' the behaviour in his or her family. The family is consequently 'an "educative" group of the most fundamental kind'.

It's OK to leave out a few words if it suits your purpose, providing you show that something is missing by the use of dots (as I have just done).

It's also acceptable to add or change a word to make things make sense within your own sentence, provided that you put any additions in *square brackets*:

> Fletcher explains how a child learns 'in direct face-to-face relationships with [family members] who matter supremely'.

You may have noticed that all these short quotes are fitted neatly into the grammar and meaning of my own sentences so that you can read straight through and it all makes sense. If you find this tricky to do at first, don't worry. The simplest way to do it is to precede your quote with a colon (:) and then to give the quote without any alterations. This is not a very sophisticated practice, but it usually avoids serious mistakes. If you're studying English, however, aim to get the hang of incorporating quotes into your sentences as soon as possible.

Quoting from literature

If you are an English literature student, you are going to have to quote frequently from the texts you are studying, and there are specific rules on how this is done. This varies according to the kind of text you quote from.

NOVELS

Quoting from novels or from work by critics presents no difficulties because these are written in prose (that is, the sentences follow straight on from each other along each line). When quoting from critics, you just use the procedure I've outlined above in the section 'Quoting'. When you quote from a novel you are studying, it's important to put the page number in square brackets immediately after your quote. Your tutor may want to check on it, and will need to be able to look it up quickly. In either case, use quotation marks for short quotes within your paragraphs and indent longer ones.

POEMS

When you quote from a poem, a rough guide is that quotations of up to a line and a half can be incorporated into your own paragraphs, while those of two or more lines look better indented (see the section 'Indenting'). Aim to limit your quotes to three lines, and never quote chunks. All spellings, punctuation, and capital letters must be copied exactly, and, *when indenting, keep to the same lines as the original*. The titles of poems should be put in quotation marks when you refer to them in the body of your essay. Put the page number of a poem in square brackets immediately after the quote, just as you would with a novel.

Take special care when quoting more than one line but not indenting. You will need to use a slash (/) to show where a line ends. Here's an example taken from an undergraduate essay I wrote on William Blake's 'The Chimney Sweeper' from his book *Songs of Innocence*:

> *Tom dreams that an angel sets the child sweeps free so that 'leaping laughing they run/And wash in a river and shine in the Sun!'*

The original lines in the poem look like this:

Then down a green plain leaping laughing they run
And wash in a river and shine in the Sun!

DRAMA

It can be easier to quote from drama than from poetry, as you don't need to stick to the same line layout as shown in the text, unless, as with much of Shakespeare's work, the play is written in verse form (for which you follow the rules for quoting from poetry). You need to make clear to your reader who is speaking, but you don't need to put the character's name at the side of the page. Here's an extract from David's essay on the play *'Master Harold' ... and the Boys* by Athol Fugard (Harold is known as Hally):

> *Hally is a smart boy, but Sam, the coloured servant, is poetical as well as smart. He describes difficulties between people in terms of 'bumping' into people on a dance floor. Then he takes in the world:*
>
> Open a newspaper and what do you read? America
> has bumped into Russia, England is bumping
> into India, rich man bumps into poor man. Those are big
> collisions, Hally. They make for a lot of bruises.

In this quotation, David didn't need to note that Sam is speaking because it is quite clear from his introduction.

When quoting from a play, you will need to give act, scene and (whenever possible) line number. Here's a quote from Shakespeare's *Hamlet*. The number of the act is in upper-case Roman numerals, the scene number is in lower-case Roman numerals, and the line is in ordinary Arabic figures:

To be, or not to be, that is the question. (III.i.56)

Mentioning a writer's idea

When you refer to someone's idea or to the results of an experiment or survey that someone has conducted, you need to show clearly that the idea is not your own. You need to give the author credit for it just as you do when quoting someone's exact words.

In the essay I wrote on Fletcher's book – *The Family and Marriage in*

Britain, I needed to refer to other writers in order to discuss the ideas that Fletcher himself had put forward. I referred more than once to a writer called E. Zaretsky, who wrote a book called *Capitalism, the Family, and Personal Life.* Here's a small section of my essay:

> *Zaretsky notes that the women's movement rested on two main bases. One was the situation of late Victorian working-class wives in employment; the other was that of middle-class wives in the same era. These middle-class women who had no job, skills or property rights began to demand education and entry to the professions.*

By giving Zaretsky's name, I've shown clearly that I've taken the ideas that follow from the work of this writer. In addition to this, it was also important to get my reference and bibliography correct. In the sections below, I have set out exactly how this is done, according to which referencing system you need to use.

Plagiarism

Plagiarism is the act of using someone else's words or ideas as if they were your own. Every time you quote, or mention ideas you have gleaned from your reading (whether in a book, magazine, or on disk) or from radio, TV, film, or tape, you *must* acknowledge the writer (or speaker) and use quotation marks where relevant. If you use a spoken quote, put quotation marks (or speech marks) round the exact words just as you would if it were written text.

An essay containing plagiarized material may result in a grade of 0 being given. Clearly, it's not something worth risking. Nine times out of ten, a tutor will either know the book that has been used or will be able to spot the difference in writing style between the essay itself and unmarked quotes from another writer. So make sure that you have all your references in place. Forgetting to do that could get you in as much trouble as doing it on purpose.

References and bibliography

A **reference** is a note that you make of where you found a particular idea or a sentence or two that you have quoted. A **bibliography** is just a list of the books you've looked at in the process of preparing an assignment.

There are two different methods of recording the books you've consulted for a particular essay and your direct references and quotations from any of them. These methods are Harvard referencing and

British Standard referencing. I've set them out separately below. They are quite similar in some ways, so you need to take care not to get them mixed up. I've used the same examples in each, so if you want to compare them it will be easy to do so. I'd suggest, however, that you read only the one you need and avoid getting confused. Both systems are widely used, so you will need to check with your tutor to find which one is applicable to your subject.

It is likely, for example, that if your subject is English, you will need to use the British system, and if it is sociology or a science subject you will be using the Harvard system. It's just not possible, however, to be categorical on this. Different departments within a college – and occasionally even individual tutors – will have their own preferences. Occasionally, you will be told that either system is acceptable. I'll give below the basics for each system. There are many further refinements to each, but if you do need to know more, your tutor should be able to help. Once you are used to using a system, you can easily learn extra tricks.

The bad news is that, whichever method you use, you will need to get it *exactly* right. Every name must be correct, and every comma and full stop has to be in the right place. You'll need to spend a little time getting to grips with the system you use, but once you've got into the referencing habit, things will be quite straightforward. Do check with your tutors, however, that the punctuation I've shown is what is wanted in your particular department: there can be variations – especially in Harvard referencing.

For both methods, whenever you refer to the **title** of a book, journal, newspaper or magazine (at any point in your assignments), either underline it or, if you have a word processor, put it in italics. Put the title of an **article** – or **chapter** from a book – in quotation marks. I always use single quotation marks to differentiate from speech (for which I use double), but this is a personal preference. Single or double marks are acceptable.

The Harvard referencing system

Mentioning a writer's idea
If I use a book by Tony Buzan, I might write the following:

> *Buzan states that the brain stores images from every point in our lives and that these can be recalled. (1986)*

Here, I have stated the writer's name and his idea, so in brackets after my point I give the date of publication of the book by Buzan in which I found it.

I might decide to write slightly differently:

> *The brain stores images from every point in our lives and these can be recalled. (Buzan 1986)*

This time, I've not mentioned the writer's name, so I must give it in brackets, together with the date of publication of the book.

QUOTING FROM A WRITER

I might decide to copy part of what Buzan actually wrote:

> *It is actually possible that 'somewhere in the brain there is a vast store of perfect images and associations that does not change with time ...' (Buzan 1986: 13)*

Because I have used the writer's actual words, I must add the number of the page from which I've copied those words to the writer's name and the date of publication of the book. My dots show that I haven't quoted the whole of Buzan's sentence.

YOUR LIST OF REFERENCES

At the end of your assignment, you will need a list of the authors whose ideas you've mentioned and/or from whom you've quoted. The list must be in *alphabetical order* by authors' surnames. My reference for Buzan would appear like this:

Buzan, T. (1986), *Use Your Memory*, BBC Publications, London.

You can see from this that the order of items is as follows (I've put all the punctuation marks in bold):

surname**,** initial. **(**date**),** title**,** publisher**,** place.

It may help to be aware that, apart from full stops after initials, there is only one full stop in a Harvard reference – at the end.

If I quote from a chapter in a book that is a collection of work by different writers, the reference would appear like this:

Gilbert, S. M. (1986), 'What do feminist critics want? A postcard from the volcano' in *The New Feminist Criticism*, ed. E. Showalter, Virago Press, London, pp. 29–45.

Note the indentation after the first line to make the author's name stand out. The title of the chapter is generally put in quotation marks, but only the first word needs to start with a capital letter (unless there are names).

If I quote from an article in a magazine or journal, the reference would look like this:

Sinha, A. (1990), 'Social and spatial order in villages in India', *Landscape Research* vol. 15, no. 3, pp. 12–19.

Here, the first and last page numbers of *the entire article* appear at the end of the reference. This reference contains exact details of the issue in which the article appeared. Only the first word of the title of the article needs a capital letter – apart, of course, from names (in this case, *India*).

Your bibliography

In your bibliography, you will list all the books you've consulted *except* the ones that appear in your list of references. Like the list of references, they will be in alphabetical order by the surnames of authors.

This is where the Harvard system scores. You will use exactly the same method of setting out each item in the *bibliography* as that shown for *references*.

Reminder: do check with your tutors for local variations.

The British standard referencing system

Mentioning a writer's idea

If I use a book by Tony Buzan, I might write the following:

Buzan states that the brain stores images from every point in our lives and that these can be recalled. 1

Here, I have stated the writer's name and his idea. So I have followed my statement with a number. My next reference would be numbered 2, and so on.

I might decide to write slightly differently:

The brain stores images from every point in our lives and these can be recalled. 1

Although I've not given the writer's name this time, I deal with this item in exactly the same way as when he was mentioned – that is, I put a number immediately after my sentence.

QUOTING FROM A WRITER
I might decide to copy part of what Buzan actually wrote:

> Buzan states that it is actually possible that 'somewhere in the brain there is a vast store of perfect images and associations that does not change with time ...' 1

As you can see, this, too, is done in the same manner as those examples above. I just put a number immediately after the quote. My dots there show that I haven't quoted the whole of Buzan's sentence.

YOUR LIST OF REFERENCES
At the end of your assignment, you will need a list of the authors whose ideas you've mentioned and/or from whom you've quoted. The list will be in numerical order, starting at 1, and each item on it will link to the numbers you've given in your assignment. So your references in this section will be in *exactly the same order* as the statements, acknowledgements and quotes that appear in the body of your work. My reference for Buzan would look like this:

1 Tony Buzan, *Use Your Memory*, p. 13.

I have used the writer's first name rather than an initial because that is what appears on the cover of the book. If the name on the cover was *T. Buzan*, I'd have written that in my reference.

The order of items in the reference is as follows (I've put all the punctuation marks in bold):

First name surname**,** title**,** page number**.**

It may help to be aware that there are two commas and one full stop in every *simple* British Standard reference. All the details, therefore, are given in *one sentence*.

If I quote from a chapter in a book that is a collection of work by different writers, the reference would appear like this:

5 Sandra M. Gilbert, 'What do Feminist Critics Want? A Postcard from the Volcano', in Elaine Showalter (ed.), *The New Feminist Criticism*, p. 34.

The details here are all given within one sentence (as in the shorter reference, above), but there are more commas.

If I quote from an article in a magazine or journal, the reference would look like this:

7 Amita Sinha, 'Social and spatial order in villages in India', in *Landscape Research*, Vol. 15 No. 3, Winter 1990, p. 17.

This reference contains exact details of the issue in which the article appeared.

YOUR BIBLIOGRAPHY

In your bibliography, you will list all the books you've consulted, *including* the ones that appear in your list of references. Unlike the references, they will be in alphabetical order by the surnames of authors. Buzan's book would appear like this:

Buzan, Tony. *Use Your Memory*. London: BBC Publications, 1986.

You can see from this that the order of items is as follows (I've put all the punctuation marks in bold):

surname**,** first name (or initial)**.** title**.** place**:** publisher**,** date**.**

It may help to be aware that there are three full stops in every item that appears in a British Standard bibliography. These separate name, title, and publishing details. There are always commas after the surname and the publisher, and a colon after the place.

If I have looked at or given a quote from a chapter in a book that is a collection of work by different writers, the entry in my bibliography would appear like this:

Gilbert, Sandra M. 'What do Feminist Critics Want? A Postcard from the Volcano' in Elaine Showalter (ed.), *The New Feminist Criticism*. London: Virago Press, 1986, pp. 29–45.

If I have looked at or given a quote from an article in a magazine or journal, the entry in my bibliography would appear like this:

> Sinha, A. 'Social and spatial order in villages in India'. *Landscape Research* Vol. 15 no. 3 (Winter 1990) pp. 12–19.

Here, *the first and last page numbers of the entire article* appear at the end of the entry. The letters *pp* stand for *pages*.

Despite the extra information needed for entries relating to chapters or journal articles, there are still just three full stops in each entry in a British Standard bibliography (apart from stops after initials and abbreviations).

SUMMARY

This chapter has covered:

▶ **Taking notes: in classes or lectures and from books**
- mind maps
- patterns
- colour
- pictures
- diagrams
- highlighting
- listing
- boxing
- ringing
- arrows for linking
- underlining
- abbreviations
- key words and sentences

▶ **Quoting**
- indenting
- quoting from literature
- referencing and bibliographies
- the Harvard referencing system
- the British Standard referencing system

8 Writing More Complex Sentences: Clauses

INTRODUCTION

If you have read the section on 'Commas' in chapter 3, you will already have some idea on how it is possible to vary the meaning and impact of what we write. Learning something about clauses will help you to

- learn to write in a more sophisticated manner
- cope with some of the complexities of academic writing.

The first part of this chapter will focus on a basic explanation of clauses. The second part will look at some examples of how students have coped with complex sentence structures. It is not always necessary to understand how clauses work in order to write well. Some people just seem to have a strong instinct for how to construct complex work. What is true, however, is that an understanding of clauses will enable you to have greater control over what you write. A further spin-off is an improved ability to think clearly, which is a real bonus.

I am not suggesting that you aim to sound very long-winded and formal. The best writers vary their sentence structure, sometimes following a complex sentence with a very short one. This adds balance and interest to a piece of work.

You won't need to worry about being tested on clauses unless you are studying linguistics (in which case you will need a more detailed book anyway). The purpose of this chapter is to enable you to get a sense of how a sentence can be composed of a number of working parts. A less publicized benefit is the effect on reading. When you are reading complex work, you can use your knowledge of clause analysis to help you understand what is meant – that is, to spot quickly which are the key (or main) statements and which are less important.

What I'll give here is a simple introduction to clauses. It will be based on traditional grammar. It can take a while to become familiar with clause analysis, so aim to get a broad understanding rather than trying to learn things off pat.

The analysis of grammar is itself currently changing, and some grammarians are starting to analyse language in new ways. Parts of the old method of clause analysis are thought to be restrictive. So I'll also show you some of the new ideas as well as traditional clause analysis.

I TRADITIONAL CLAUSE ANALYSIS

▶ Main verbs and main clauses

In a nutshell, a clause is a group of words containing a working verb and its subject. In chapter 2, I explained that it is essential for every sentence to have a working verb. Look at the following sentence:

My dog Rex fancies the cat.

The working verb is, of course, *fancies*, and the subject is *My dog Rex*. This is a simple sentence consisting of one clause.

It also became clear in chapter 2 that a sentence may have more than one verb. When a sentence contains more than one working verb (and there may be several), one of them will be more important than the others. It's called the **main verb**. (There is a minor exception to this, but I'll go into that a little further on.)

Look at the following sentence. The verbs are in bold type:

My dog Rex **fancies** the cat who often **sleeps** in the dog basket.

Because there are two working verbs here, there are two parts to the sentence:

1 My dog Rex fancies the cat

2 who often sleeps in the dog basket

I'm sure you can see that the first part of the sentence is more important than the second. The words *who often sleeps in the dog basket* just give us some extra information about the behaviour of the cat. The main focus here is on the behaviour of the dog. So the main verb in the sentence is *fancies*. The subject is *My dog Rex*.

The part of the sentence which contains the main verb is called the **main clause**. So the main clause in that sentence is:

My dog Rex fancies the cat

A main clause could always stand alone as a sentence, and we saw this clause functioning as a simple sentence at the beginning of this section.

▶ Subordinate clauses

The name given to any other group of words containing a working verb in a sentence is a **subordinate clause**. So *who often sleeps in the dog basket* is a subordinate clause.

The following sentence contains two working verbs (which are in bold type). This means that there must be two clauses:

John **was** cross with his dog because it **had eaten** the pie.

The main clause – or statement – is:

John was cross with his dog.

The second clause,

because it had eaten the pie

is a subordinate clause because it gives us some extra information which is less important here than the main statement. This sentence *focuses* on John's feelings towards his dog.

Now you might feel that loss of the pie is crucial and therefore more significant than how John felt about it. That pie may well have been John's dinner. The issue here is my intention as the writer of the sentence. I want to stress John's anger. The fact that the second clause begins with the word *because* shows that it contains an *explanation* rather than a straightforward statement of the situation.

This sentence could be lengthened by adding more clauses (the verbs are in bold):

` John **was** cross with his dog because it **had eaten** the pie which Sarah **had made**.

Even though he **is** an easy-going man, John **was** cross with his dog because it **had eaten** the pie which Sarah **had made.**

Even though he **is** an easy-going man who **loves** animals, John **was** cross with his dog because it **had eaten** the pie which Sarah **had made.**

Even though he **is** an easy-going man who **loves** animals, John **was** cross with his dog because it **had eaten** the pie which Sarah **had made** while he **had been repairing** the car.

We now have a sentence with six working verbs in it. That means that there are six clauses – one main and five subordinate. Here, the main clause is still *John was cross with his dog*. All the other clauses merely help to explain the situation. The main clause could stand alone as a fully functioning sentence. It makes sense by itself. Subordinate clauses, however, can't stand alone because they don't make sense by themselves. You may remember something of this from the first section of chapter 2.

I'll list the subordinate clauses:

Even though he **is** an easy-going man
who **loves** animals
because it **had eaten** the pie
which Sarah **had made**
while he **had been repairing** the car

Introductory words
Subordinate clauses can often be spotted by means of the words that introduce them. The following are frequently used:

although	while	since
even though	despite	unless
if	which	until
because	where	

▶ **Changing the emphasis**

Can you spot the main clause in the following sentence?

> I love chips, even though the fat is bad for me and I gain weight every time I eat them.

The most important thing I'm telling you here is that I'm very keen on chips. The main clause is *I love chips* and the main verb is *love*.

There are three more working verbs here: *is*, *gain* and *eat*. So there are three subordinate clauses:

> even though the fat **is** bad for me
> and I **gain** weight
> every time I **eat** them

Now, just as with John and the pie, you may not agree with me here. You may feel that gaining weight is the most important thing I've mentioned. In my sentence, however, I wanted to *foreground* the information that I'm keen on chips. I wanted the other points to appear less important – that is, subordinate.

If I wanted to stress the point on weight gain, I would need to construct the sentence slightly differently in order to put the *focus* on weight:

> I **gain** weight every time I **eat** chips, although I **tell** myself that it **does**n't matter and that a little fat **won't hurt** me.

Now, the main clause is

> I **gain** weight

and there are four subordinate clauses:

> every time I eat chips
> although I tell myself
> that it doesn't matter
> and that a little fat won't hurt me

You'll notice here that the chips are now in a subordinate clause. The ability to place your emphasis exactly where you want it is a very valuable skill. It can help make your writing both precise and forceful.

Those words *foreground* and *focus* are keys to finding the main clause in a sentence. When you are reading, watch out for the writer's personal view or slant on what he or she has written. A writer's focus may not be what you expect or agree with.

ACTIVITY 1

It's very useful to be able to spot the main clause in a sentence, so try your hand at underlining the **main clause** in each of the following sentences. (It will not always be at the beginning of the sentence).

1 There are fairies at the bottom of my garden where I haven't cut the grass.
2 Although it's freezing, I refuse to wear woolly undies.
3 Place all gallstones in the bucket provided after you have sewn up the patient.
4 Coming out of the supermarket, I bumped into a small horse.
5 A problem shared is a problem halved, as long as the trouble is either legal or is not divulged to a serving police officer.
6 It's hot.

▶ Co-ordinate clauses

You may remember that I suggested above that there can sometimes be more than one main clause in a sentence. It's easy to spot these because they will be linked by the words *and*, *but* or *or*:

My dog Rex **fancies** the cat *and* he **hates** the hamster.

The customer **gave** me an odd look, *but* he **said** nothing.

You **can study** in the library *or* you **can go** home.

If you think for a moment, you will see that in each sentence, the two clauses have the same value – they are each as important as the other. So we call them **co-ordinate clauses**.

Subordinate clauses, as well as main clauses, can be co-ordinate if they are linked by those words *and*, *but* or *or*:

After you **have added** all the ingredients *and* **put** the mixture in the tin, **bake** the cake for an hour and a half.

Main clause: **bake** the cake for an hour and a half
Subordinate clauses: After you **have added** all the ingredients and **put** the mixture in the tin

There are co-ordinate subordinate clauses in my sentence about the chips:

even though the fat **is** bad for me *and* I **gain** weight

There are also co-ordinate subordinate clauses in the *revised* sentence on chips:

that it **doesn't matter** *and* that a little fat **won't hurt** me

► Types of subordinate clause

There are various different types of subordinate clause in traditional analysis. The main ones are **nominal, adjectival** and **adverbial clauses**. I'm not going to cover them in great detail or set out any activities on them. If you are still interested after you have read the following, you will need to follow this up in a book that focuses solely on grammar.

NOMINAL CLAUSES
These are sometimes called noun clauses because the whole clause functions as an item as if it were one noun. In this way, a nominal clause can act as the subject of a verb. If you look back at chapter 2, you will find that we've already covered these briefly as 'extended subjects'.

ADJECTIVAL CLAUSES
These are sometimes known as relative clauses. Just like an adjective, an adjectival clause qualifies a noun or pronoun, like this:

The athlete *who won the race* was accused of taking steroids.

That is the girl *whose father won the lottery*.

Josh bought the book *which Ray had recommended.*

The nouns that each of those clauses qualifies (or describes) are *athlete, girl* and *book.*
   Adjectival clauses usually begin with one of the following words:

which, that, who, whose

Sometimes, a preposition comes first:

This is the boat *in which the refugees sailed.*

Those are the people *with whom Nelson Mandela had discussions.*

The words *where* and *when* can also sometimes be used to begin adjectival clauses:

I saw the house *where she used to live.*

It was the day *when the factory burnt down.*

ADVERBIAL CLAUSES

If you've remembered that adverbs describe verbs, you may be thinking that perhaps adverbial clauses do the same. You'd be right. (Like adverbs, they can also describe – that is, qualify – adjectives). As well as describing *working* verbs, however, they can describe infinitives as well.
   Adverbial clauses can tell us about a long list of different types of information: time, place, manner, reason, purpose, conditions, results, concessions and comparison. It's easiest to follow the first two:

I'll make some coffee *when I've finished this report.*   **time**

The phone rang *while I was painting the bathroom.*   **time**

I planted the apple tree *where we can see it from
the window.*   **place**

Put your things down *wherever you can find a space.*   **place**

Typical words for introducing some of the other types of adverbial clause are:

> because, as, since, if, unless, whether, although

▶ Phrases

Phrases are easier to understand than clauses. In traditional grammar, a phrase is a group of words that obviously fit together but do *not* include a working verb. A phrase is often part of a clause. In the sentences below, phrases are in bold type:

> Seth moored his boat **at the edge of the lake**.

> **Tomorrow morning**, I'll start painting the dining room.

> The boys were playing football, **despite the rain**.

Note that these three sentences are each composed of a single main clause, even though in two of them the phrase is separated from the main statement by a comma.

There's a phrase in that long sentence about John and his pie-eating dog:

> an easy-going man

and another in the sentence about Rex:

> in the dog basket

II SOME MODERN ANALYSIS

This section is for those who would like some idea of new trends in analysis.

▶ Non-finite clauses

If you read the final section in chapter 2, you may remember that the *technical* name for a working verb is a **finite verb**. The word *finite* really means having boundaries. You'll remember that the *name* of a verb is called the *infinitive*. There's an obvious link with the word *infinity*. An infinitive has no boundaries – it cannot be used to show us when something happens. So a working – or finite verb – is one which is doing a job and showing us something happening at a particular time. We have said that every clause contains a finite verb. Well, now I'm going to turn that on its head.

First of all, remind yourself of *subjects* and *objects* from chapter 2. Then look at the following sentence:

> The cat tried to kill a very large rat.

You can see that *tried* is a working - or finite – verb, and *to kill*, of course, is an infinitive. Traditional analysis would say that since there is just one finite verb in this sentence – *tried* – it consists of just one clause.

Now some grammarians would analyse this sentence like this:

The cat tried	main clause (finite verb – *tried*)
to kill a very large rat	non-finite clause – in this case, an **infinitive clause**

Some people would argue that *to kill a very large rat* is a clause because, even though it hasn't got a finite verb, you can say that the verb *to kill* has a direct object here – *a very large rat*.

Take care, however, that you don't go the whole hog and start writing sentences completely lacking in finite verbs – not even in the light of what I'll show you next.

▶ Verbless clauses

This one looks like a complete contradiction in terms because I've spent quite a bit of time banging on about every clause having a verb. Anyway, try this:

> Fearless as a tiger, the cat bludgeoned the rat.

A modern grammarian might analyse that sentence like this:

> the cat bludgeoned the rat – main clause (finite verb –
> *bludgeoned*)
> Fearless as a tiger –   verbless clause

Those words *Fearless as a tiger* might be seen to constitute a clause on the grounds that, in this particular sentence, they actually mean: *the cat was fearless as a tiger*. The verb *was* is therefore seen to be *implied* in the words *fearless as a tiger*. So we can pretend that the finite verb is there.

▶ Plural-verb main clauses

This is almost the opposite of finding a clause that has no stated verb. In this type of sentence, a subordinate clause is said to be a part of the main clause. Like this:

> Some scientists argue that the earth's climate is changing.

Even though there are two finite verbs here, some modern grammarians would say that it is misleading to try to split the sentence into two clauses. They would insist that the words *that the earth's climate is changing* cannot be divorced from the verb *argue* without harming the meaning.

This would seem to make very good sense when applied to my revised sentence about chips. The clause

> although I tell myself

sounds a little odd. It looks much clearer when put with the following statement:

> although I tell myself that it doesn't matter

This is just a taster of modern analysis. You can see that things may get very complicated. The most important thing to take from this chapter, however, is a sense of the structure of sentences and the knowledge that meaning will alter according to the way in which a sentence is structured.

III EXAMPLES OF UNDERGRADUATE WORK

Here are two examples of work by George, an Open University student. I've put the verbs in bold so that you can more easily spot the separate clauses:

from an essay on music:

> There **are** three distinct phases in Beethoven's music: the early work where he **conveyed** fundamental and universal experiences, the middle period in which he **focused** on achievement through heroism despite suffering, and a later period (the period of the last quartets) in which suffering no longer **plays** the same part and something new **is being communicated**.

We can analyse that sentence like this:

There are three distinct phases in Beethoven's music
   main clause
the early work where he conveyed . . . experiences
   subordinate clause
the middle period in which he focused . . . suffering
   subordinate clause
and a later period . . . no longer plays the same part
   subordinate clause
and something new is being communicated
   subordinate co-ordinate clause

The use of subordinate clauses allows George to write in a more sophisticated manner than if he had used a more simple construction with short sentences, like this:

> There are three distinct phases in Beethoven's music. In his early work, he conveyed fundamental and universal experiences. In his middle period, he focused on achievement through heroism despite suffering. In his later period (the period of the last quartets) suffering no longer plays the same part and something new is being communicated.

There is absolutely nothing wrong with this more simple treatment; but in the sentence that uses the subordinate clauses, George seems to have more control over the material, and it is more satisfying to read.

You may find it helpful to see how the long sentence can be shown as a simple table:

> There are three distinct phases in Beethoven's music:
> the early work . . .
> the middle period . . .
> and a later period . . .

This demonstrates the underlying scaffolding of the sentence. If you are having trouble getting an idea on paper, it's actually possible to put it down in diagram form first and construct a sentence from the diagram. If you work backwards from the diagram of George's points on Beethoven to the sentence he wrote, you can see how it's possible to include points as you go along by means of subordinate clauses.

from an essay on architecture in the 1920s and 1930s

> *The architect Mies van der Rohe, who **used** the International style vocabulary of flat roofs, white walls, windows flush with walls to suggest volume, and the visible continuous steel supports which **were** part of Le Corbusier's architectural vocabulary of expressed structure, **created** a block of flats which **were** later **copied** all over Berlin.*

There is a great deal of information packed into this sentence. The effect, again, is of control. In this particular example, the main clause is split into two sections, and that is fine. The analysis is as follows:

> The architect Mies van der Rohe **created** a block of flats
>   main clause
> who **used** the International style . . . steel supports
>   subordinate clause
> which **were** part . . . expressed structure
>   subordinate clause
> which **were** later **copied** all over Berlin
>   subordinate clause

Note: the last clause does not contain two verbs but one verb split apart by the adverb *later*.

I hope you can see that, by using those introductory words *who* and *which,* George was able to build up a highly complex sentence without too much difficulty.

Of course, you are not likely to want to have to think hard about clauses all the time you are writing your essays. Just be aware that it's possible to write longer and more complex sentences and have a go at it every now and then. You may in fact already be writing complex sentences but having a few problems with them. Keep in mind the idea of a table or diagram, and have a go at analysing one or two of your own sentences. This will help to give you a 'feel' for construction.

SUMMARY

This chapter has covered:

- main clause — the most important statement in a sentence
- main verb — the working verb in the main clause
- subordinate clause — a clause that contains less important information
- co-ordinate clause — a clause (either main or subordinate) that has the same value as its partner clause
- nominal, adjectival and adverbial clauses
- phrase — a group of words *without* a working verb
- modern clause analysis: — non-finite clauses
  verbless clauses
  plural-verb main clauses
- changing your focus
- putting your points in diagram form

Part Three
Writing for Other Purposes

9 Style and Summaries

INTRODUCTION

If you are a student, you will not be writing merely essays. You may be asked to write summaries, reports, articles, letters, and even to do some creative writing. The remaining chapters of this book (except for the chapter on writing in exams) cover various types of assignment that you may be given. This chapter forms a basis for each of the others.

At first glance, it might seem a little strange for style and summaries to sit together in a chapter, but there's method in my madness. Many courses nowadays require students to be able to write in ways appropriate to specific written forms and to particular kinds of reader. The AQA (Assessment and Qualifications Alliance, formerly the Associated Examining Board) currently combines this work with summary-writing in its A-level exams, and I've found this to be a very useful combination. It gives people really good practice in focusing on the specific *purpose* of a piece of writing and on the *readers* for whom it is designed.

This chapter is split into three sections: I Style; II Basic summary-writing; and III Summaries for specific purposes.

If you are in a hurry to find out how to write a brief résumé of a piece of writing, turn straight to section II. You might like to work on your style when you have more time. Section I is much longer than the others and covers:

- simplicity – with examples on writing instructions and describing a process
- tone – with an explanation of persuasive writing
- register – with examples on language suitable for specific tasks.

I STYLE

The word *style* has different uses. It can refer to a person's particular way of writing, to the type of writing needed for a particular piece of work, or to writing well. When a writer specializes in one form of writing – for example, poetry, novels or even newspaper articles – he or she will inevitably develop a very individual style which others can often spot without being given the writer's name. This kind of thing grows slowly. You may already have a style that shows up strongly in your work. The more writing you do, the more your own style will emerge. This chapter is concerned with showing how to make improvements to the general *texture* of your writing and demonstrating how you can write in very different ways to suit the purpose of a particular piece of work.

Good writing can be developed in several ways. One of these is to make sure that you read well-written material. Whatever your subject, the more you vary your reading, the better. Go for novels, travel-writing, biographies, broadsheet newspapers, and anything else that you come across. Follow your own particular interests, and, from time to time, challenge yourself with some difficult reading material. All this will gradually have a spin-off effect on your own work.

▶ Simplicity and clarity

One of the key ways to improve your style is to aim constantly for simplicity and clarity. The best writing is easy to read and uses contemporary (rather than out of date) vocabulary. Sometimes, students feel that they are expected to aim for language that sounds important or very formal. This really is not the case. Of course, the writing in some textbooks can seem really dense and difficult, but that doesn't mean that it's written in a style worth copying. Don't call a spade 'an implement for turning earth'.

The best writing states its case in the simplest possible terms. This doesn't mean leaving things out or omitting to use technical words when they are essential. It means that we need to avoid all unnecessary jargon and to give sufficient explanation in order to be clearly understood. It also means that we must use punctuation and paragraphing to help the reader along (see chapters 3 and 6).

Checklist for simplicity

- *use a short word* rather than a long one
- *be yourself:* don't copy style from another writer
- *write the truth* as you see it
- *check your logic* – have you said what you mean?
- *be as brief as possible* without omitting essential points
- *omit clichés* (e.g. 'in this day and age', 'the bottom line')
- *use active verbs* rather than passive (see chapter 1)
- *use concrete nouns* rather than abstract whenever possible (see chapter 4)
- *use helpful punctuation and paragraphing*

Look at this example of long-winded writing:

> *Many of the somewhat extended psychoanalytic case notes written and published by Sigmund Freud have become the subject of castigation by feminist writers.*

There's absolutely no need to say that Freud's work was *psychoanalytic* because everyone knows that. There's certainly no need to say that it was *written and published*. The words *the subject of castigation* can be reduced considerably, and we only need one word for *feminist writers*. The piece would be much more readable like this:

> Freud's work has been attacked by feminists.

This new sentence gets straight to the point and won't send a reader to sleep. The original sentence makes a really good sedative. You may have noticed that the verb is passive. In this case, I'm not worried about that because I want to focus here on Freud rather than on the feminists. If I wished, however, I could change it to:

> Feminists have attacked Freud's work.

The words you use need to be the right ones for the job in hand. This will mean, of course, that when you are writing essays, it will be essential for you to use certain technical terms. If it's possible to use simple language, however, always do so.

Finding the right word

If you have a *good dictionary* and a *thesaurus* (which will give you a choice of words for non-technical items and save you repeating yourself) you will have the right tools for the job. Get the best dictionary you can afford. It will pay dividends in the long run. A thesaurus can be very handy for searching out a word that says *exactly* what you mean.

The dictionary will help you not just with spelling but with accuracy. People often use a word that means more or less what they intend, but not quite. Every now and then, you might try checking the definition of a word you think you are quite sure of. This can be quite an eye-opener. It's surprising how many times a dictionary definition turns out to be not quite what we expect. A good deal of your checking, however, can be done by just thinking carefully. Look at the example below from Susan's essay for her Access course – 'Discuss the proposition that education is wasted on the young':

> *A reason why this proposition may be feasible is the way in which attending school is enforced.*

The word *feasible* relates to possibility. It is perfectly possible to make *any* proposition. A word that would fit much better here is *valid*. What Katy meant was that the proposition could be shown to be in some ways convincing.

You can see from this that finding the right word can sometimes take a little time; but it's time well spent because your work will have greater strength and your command of the language will be constantly improving.

Writing instructions

Very often, students returning to education are given an assignment on writing instructions. This gives people particularly good practice in making a piece of writing really clear. Before you begin this type of work, check carefully whether what is wanted is a set of bullet points (like my list below) or writing done in full sentences and paragraphs. A list of bullet points gives just the bare bones of a piece of information. I've used the system here and there throughout this book to draw your attention to specific points.

I'd guess that there have been countless times when you've been baffled by instructions and have muttered dire things about the person who wrote them. The problem usually relates to one or more of the following:

- information missed out
- information not clearly explained
- language for the initiated only – i.e. jargon or abbreviations
- confusion caused by incorrect grammar and/or punctuation

Some of us complain bitterly about the instructions in computer manuals. It can be particularly galling to find that somebody who herself understands computers has absolutely no trouble with the manuals. This can happen in any field, however. When we understand a subject, we tend to forget that people without inside knowledge will need to have things spelt out for them. Here's an example of an instruction that often baffles me:

Take three a day with a main meal.

Now how many times a day would I be taking those tablets? Three times? Or can I take them all in one go? It does say *three* with *a* main meal. And should I take them before, during or after the meal?

Let's improve the instruction:

Take one tablet before a main meal three times a day.

That's a bit better. I've seen this one scores of times. But I eat only one main meal a day. I wouldn't call my breakfast toast or my lunchtime sandwich a main meal. Does this mean that I must increase my food intake while I'm on those pills? Writing clear instructions is not necessarily a straightforward business.

The readership for instructions on a bottle of pills includes *all* adults (and probably quite a lot of younger people too). When writing instructions for something that could be used throughout the population, we must make no assumptions about readers' prior knowledge or understanding – except to hope that they can understand simple English. Of course, the need for translations in today's multicultural society is another issue altogether.

There's a really good exercise for practising writing clear instructions which you may already have been asked to do in one form or another:

Write two or three paragraphs explaining how to go on foot from one destination to another a short distance away – say, five or ten minutes' walk – in a place you know well. You might choose to start at a point in your local town and finish at a particular room in your college. Do this as if for someone who knows absolutely nothing of the area.

You will find that you have to focus very clearly on getting your instructions just right. If you are studying with a friend, see if he or she thinks it would be possible to follow your instructions without having any prior knowledge of the area.

A good place to look for examples of how to give clear instructions is a simple cookery book. Here you will nearly always find each step of a process very clearly explained. Something like a car manual is not usually quite so helpful because these books usually expect readers to have a good knowledge of the subject.

Describing a process

This is really very similar to writing instructions except that it often relates to something that has already taken place – like a scientific experiment. As with instructions on a bottle of pills, accuracy is essential. Whatever your subject, aim to make your descriptions so clear that they could be understood by someone who knew nothing whatever about the topic. This will mean giving very accurate descriptions and not assuming that an item is so simple that everyone will understand it. Here's an example – putting oil in my Mini:

> *Before I begin, I must make sure that the car is on level ground and that it has been stationary for about half an hour. First, I unhook the catch on the car's bonnet. Then I raise the bonnet, pull out the attached rod that will support it while I work, and clip the end of the rod in place at the left-hand side. Next, I take the dipstick out of its socket. The dipstick is a long rod that can be spotted by its curved handle. This is easy to reach as it is right at the front of the car. I then wipe the oily end of the dipstick with a rag or tissue and replace it in its socket.*

> *Then I remove the dipstick again and check the level of oil on it. There are* maximum *and* minimum *marks at the lower end of the dipstick. If the oil level is below maximum, I replace the stick, remove the oil filler cap, which is situated on the top of the engine, just behind the dipstick socket, and pour in a little oil. I wait a couple of minutes for the oil to settle, and then recheck the level using the dipstick again. I now add more oil if the level is still below maximum.*

I then replace the filler cap and make sure that it is fully tightened. Then I release the bonnet rod from its catch, clip it back into place, and carefully close the bonnet, making sure (with a final push) that it is securely fixed.

The first thing to notice here is the amount of detail included that will appear superfluous to anyone who is used to changing oil. The second thing you might look at is how often I reuse a noun in places where we might normally use a pronoun. For example, in the second sentence, I used the word *rod* twice instead of using the word *it* on the second occasion. The reason for this is that I needed to make things crystal clear for anyone who has never changed oil before. This sentence already contains the word *it* which refers to *bonnet*. If I'd used *it* again, the unsuspecting reader might assume that this, too, referred to *bonnet*.

When doing this kind of writing, it can help considerably if you can *visualize* the process. This will help you to incorporate minor items that might get overlooked.

▶ Tone

Using an appropriate tone is important for all types of writing. Tone is easiest to spot in spoken language. We know at once if someone sounds friendly, upset or impatient. We often react strongly to tone. You may at one time or another have said to someone, "I don't like your tone." We constantly vary our tone of voice. When talking to a baby, my voice is likely to be gentle and friendly. If someone spills coffee over me, I may sound shocked and cross. If I talk about holidays I had as a child, I'll start getting nostalgic.

Tone shows up in written language too, but here it can be a bit harder to spot. Understanding how it functions, however, will make you more able to control tone in your own writing. When writing essays and most other assignments, you just need to watch that you don't start getting emotional about your subject matter, because this might indicate that you were biased. A good essay shows various sides of an issue and comes to a cool, logical conclusion.

In letters, too, it's best to keep calm, whatever the issues involved. In letters to friends and family, of course, you can let your hair down and be as biased as you like. Most of us like to know what our friends *feel* about things. Once you've mastered the technique, however, you can have fun writing sophisticated letters to newspapers in a variety of tones. Here is the final paragraph of a letter to *The Independent* on hardships endured by British farmers. It uses a rather scathing tone to get its message across:

> *Last year, [1999] grain and early potatoes achieved the same ex-farm prices, in actual pounds not real terms, as in 1979 and 1970 respectively. Why don't politicians and civil servants copy the farmers and return to 1970s salaries? Why don't they work a seven-day week with few days off in a year? It would take three public servants to replace each farmer just to keep the countryside neat and tidy.*

And here's an extract from a letter with a very ironic tone. It refers both to the arguments on importing GM foods and to certain agricultural disagreements between Britain and France:

> *So the new international agreement on GM foods is a triumph for Michael Meacher* [Minister for the Environment]. *All countries will now have the right to ban food they think will harm them without needing to go through the tedious process of justifying the ban with scientific evidence before an independent tribunal ... . Funny, but I could have sworn that when the French claimed this right recently it was vigorously opposed by Britain.*

Persuasive writing

Persuasive writing entails using another kind of tone. The object is to get readers on your side. It's important therefore, not to overdo things or appear belligerent. The ability to write persuasively is a very handy skill.

This kind of writing is really very simple. If you want to get someone to agree with your point of view or to take a particular action, you need to:

- show the positive features of your idea
- omit or play down any negative aspects
- push your points strongly
- appear to be committed
- take care not to offend.

This is in addition, of course, to writing simply and clearly. What follows is some work by Joan, a student on an Access to Higher

Education course. Joan's assignment was to write a 750-word paper for the governors of her local community college on *The need for an Access building on the main college site*. The students on Joan's course were having to spend a great deal of time travelling between two sites. They all felt strongly, however Joan makes her points forcefully but without obvious emotion. She writes with a committed tone. You can see that she comes across as feeling strongly about the validity of her argument and as someone who has thought carefully about the issues and is prepared to stand up for what she believes. Here is her opening paragraph:

> *Access courses are an increasingly essential part of academic life in Britain. With job insecurity, and the growing realization that a person will need several careers during his working life, Access is on its way to becoming as established as any other part of adult training. Many benefit-recipients, especially single parents, are being given full encouragement to find careers for themselves. Access is becoming the primary route. But in this area of the country, space must be made for it, that is – physical space.*

Notice how Joan uses this paragraph to set the scene. She focuses on the current situation for Access students in Britain, and underlines this by showing that the government clearly wishes single parents to undertake training for work. Her final sentence then gets straight to the main issue.

Here is one of Joan's central paragraphs where she accentuates positive aspects of her suggestions:

> *With thorough planning, costs can be kept to a minimum – but it's not all about spending money. The building can be made to pay for its own upkeep by being hired out for local activities: evening classes, day classes, local drama and music groups. The surrounding area abounds with different groups that need space in order to function.*

Her final paragraph pushes hard to get her points across. Her commitment is especially evident here:

> *None of this can happen with the present arrangement. With only three subjects on offer, and basic facilities too far away, the current Access course is undermined and disadvantaged. It cannot become fully effective for the community it serves, or for the college.*

Joan leaves the reader in no doubt of her views. She makes a compelling case. You can see, however, that, although she hammers her points home, she is *consistently polite*. Since this paper was aimed at college governors, it is also fairly formal.

▶ Register

When we talk to someone, we generally automatically adjust our language for the needs of the particular listener. This is called changing **register.** When talking to a baby, we will use simple words. When we speak to a priest or other religious person, we are likely to use fairly formal language and to take care not to use words that might offend. At a football ground, the talk will be full of football terminology. There are many situations where traditional language is used. In wedding services, for instance, many of the words spoken have remained unchanged for hundreds of years.

If I turn from talking to a baby to making a phone call about my gas bill, you can be pretty certain that I will have changed register. When we write, we need to follow a similar procedure and adjust our language to the particular task in hand.

ACTIVITY 1

Have a brief look at the four extracts printed below and see if you can jot down a few notes on the type of language used in each. For example, you might feel that it is formal, religious, simple, chatty, and so on. See if you can describe the different types of writing. I've given some feedback after the examples.

1   Disconnecting the fill hoses

Should the fill hoses need to be disconnected at any time proceed as follows:

Turn off the water supplies. Select the non-fast coloureds programme and start the machine.

Wait for a few seconds, then switch off.

This will release the pressure in the hoses so that they can be removed without spraying.

DO NOT switch off to cancel the programme. The machine will simply carry on from where it was interrupted next time you switch it on.

2 Congratulations to you both –
And warmest wishes, too,
For nothing less than happiness
That lasts a lifetime through;
For surely both of you deserve
The very finest things,
And all the deep contentment
That a happy marriage brings.

3 This offer of employment is subject to one or all of the following:

(a) The receipt of references which we find entirely satisfactory;

(b) The LEA's* Occupational Health Physician being satisfied as to your medical fitness for the post;

(c) Satisfactory LEA checks including those required under the Provisions of the Home Office Circular 47/93 (Protection of Children).

4 **Football will be death of Scots** By Roger Dobson

SCOTTISH FOOTBALL is a dangerous game – and not just for the players. Fans of the game can end up in hospital, even those who watched Scotland's World Cup efforts from the supposed safety of their armchairs last summer.

According to a report in the *Scottish Medical Journal*, one man had to be taken to hospital after an acute asthma attack brought on by seeing Scotland lose disastrously to Morocco. Another was treated for self-inflicted deafness caused by shouting too loudly.

One fan was found unconscious dressed in full Scotland strip after apparently

---

* LEA: Local Education Authority.

overdosing on temazepam, while another needed therapy for psychoses after reporting that the Scottish team were talking to him through the TV screen. Eight other patients were treated for chest pains, two for hyperventilation, three for alcohol-related seizures and one for palpitations.

In total, Edinburgh Royal Infirmary's casualty unit treated 151 patients with football-related problems during the finals, mostly alcohol-related trauma cases involving a fall or a fight.

And the casualties are not restricted to fans: one football widow faked a fit in a desperate attempt to divert her husband's attention from a World Cup game. She was taken to the Royal Infirmary, where the medical notes on her case are succinct: "Attention-seeking behaviour, husband watching the football."
(*The Independent*, 7.8.99)

Feedback

1 The language used in the instructions for my washing machine is rather stark. There are no adjectives or descriptions of any kind. This is the language of instructions everywhere. We could even call it 'instructional language'. It is simple, clear and gets straight to the point. Notice that there are a number of commands: *Turn off*, *Select*, *Wait*, and *DO NOT switch off* ... . There are also some brief explanations. Most of the sentences are short, and there's a lot of white space on the page. This makes the whole thing very easy to read. The manufacturers don't want users to be in any doubt as to how to proceed.

Look at the nouns: *hoses*, *water supplies*, *programme*, *machine*. They all relate directly to concrete items (see chapter 4 for an explanation of nouns). There's no abstract language here – and there's no emotion.

2 The wedding card doesn't say a great deal either, but the language it uses is very different. If I'd not told you where the writing came from, you'd still instantly recognise the language of greeting cards. In contrast to the language of instructions, it focuses on feelings.

As a poem, this piece makes use of rhythm and rhyme which are very powerful devices for getting feelings across. Individual words have been chosen very carefully with the purpose of the card in mind. The aim is to send to the couple a kind of blessing on their marriage. So it focuses solely on the best possibilities: *happiness* and *contentment*; and it uses superlatives*: *warmest* and *finest*. There are no such extravagant messages in the job offer that follows.

---

* *superlative*: the highest form of a quality – e.g. warm, warmer, *warmest*; fine, finer, *finest*.

3 The language of this job offer from a local authority is so formal and carefully-worded that you might mistake it for a legal document. In fact, it is a document that could be used in a court of law if (once it has been signed and accepted) either the authority or the employee fails to stick to the agreement made between them.

Here the language is very restricted. There must be no possibility of anyone being able to find more than one meaning in these statements. If it comes to a showdown, the employer will not want to have a lawyer claiming that the words could mean anything other than what they were originally intended to mean. Notice the careful wording of the introductory clause. It states that the 'offer of employment is subject to *one or all'* (my italics) of three conditions. This allows the authority scope to demand that the employee fulfil all three criteria. This is the language of bureaucratic organizations: it is used for particular types of written evidence and for making sure that points will be understood and followed in a prescribed manner.

4 Journalism is a totally different ball game. This extract from a broadsheet newspaper is one of those short pieces that are put in to fill an empty corner. As with any piece of journalism, the writer must grab our attention straight away – as Roger Dobson does with his first six words.

The writing here is clear, sharp, and filled with facts. It uses bite-sized paragraphs (in order to keep the reader awake) and a style common to journalism around the globe. *According to a report* is a very familiar journalistic turn of phrase. Note too, the pattern built up just from referring to individual instances of trouble: *Fans of the game, one man, Another', One fan, Eight other patients.* This is actually a highly-skilled piece of writing. The humour derives almost entirely from the organization of the material. Nowhere does this writer divert from broadsheet journalism's semi-formal style or descend merely to cracking jokes.

ACTIVITY 2

Now look at the three short examples below, and see if you can work out both the register and the tone employed in each one. It doesn't matter if you don't use exactly the same words as I do. Having a go will give you practice in focusing on language and help to make you more aware of how different effects are achieved.

1 Spacious and attractive, this flat occupies a prime position in the town, overlooking the park and with extensive views from both bedrooms.

2 I, Thomas Bates, being of sound mind, do hereby bequeath ...

3 Release, anti-clockwise, the two grub screws that retain the inlet elbows, using the 2.5 mm A/F hexagon wrench (supplied).

My answers are on p. 272. Don't worry if you found this a little tricky. The main thing is to get a handle on the general concept: you need to be aware that we write in very different ways according to subject matter, situation, and the people we're communicating with. I'm sure you can see that it wouldn't be helpful to write instructions for the use of a washing machine in the language of a wedding card – and vice versa. That's an obvious example, of course; you might like to use it as a reminder when you have a specific writing task to do.

II BASIC SUMMARY-WRITING

As a student, whenever you are asked to summarize anything, you will almost certainly be told how long your summary should be. You might, for example, be asked to summarize the main points of a book on one side of A4 paper. After reading the book, you'd need to make a list of the main issues. Then you would put them in a useful order, explaining each very briefly. You might use the contents and any information given on the book's dust jacket to help you here. If you were really pushed for time, you might even be able to produce a passable summary from these sources without even reading the book!

You may, however, be asked to produce a summary of something much shorter – an article, perhaps, or just a couple of pages from a textbook. A good summary of this type will include everything of any importance from the original. The trick here is to disentangle the key points from explanations, examples, and blatant diversions. There are distinct stages in writing a good summary, and it's very important to stick to them:

1 A first quick read.
2 Note-making.
3 Writing a first draft.
4 Checking your word-count and editing.
5 Writing your final draft.

1 Your first reading will familiarize you with the material and so make you a little more comfortable about the task ahead. You will also begin to get a feel for the central issues.

2 Your notes will form the basis of your summary, so you need to take great care at this stage. You will need to copy out any technical terms, but, in general, you will need to translate the original material into *your own words*. This is crucial. If you use the writer's words, you will not be able to demonstrate your understanding of the piece and you will have great difficulty in keeping your summary to the required length without leaving out important material.

3 Your first draft should be written from your notes. Try not to look back at the original while you are writing. If you have managed to use your own words throughout your notes, this draft really will have your stamp on it. You will not sound as though you are merely parroting what you've read. Aim to keep this draft short, but don't worry too much about word-counts at this stage. The mind can't cope with two complex processes at the same time.

4 If you have been given a word limit, you'll probably have to spend some time cutting out words and phrases that are not wholly necessary. In certain A-level English exams, it is the practice to count the words in a candidate's summary and then to ignore any words that go beyond the limit given. So don't risk having part of your summary deleted. Editing will depend partly on the instructions you've been given: your writing may just need tidying up a little.

If, by any chance, your summary is *much shorter* than the word limit, it's probable that you have omitted too much. Check your notes against the original, and add extra points to your summary.

5 Just copy out your edited version.

If you have faithfully followed the five steps, you can't go far wrong. Problems with summary-writing are nearly always the result of rushing stage 2. It really is essential to get down *all the key points* and to get them down in *your own words* as far as possible.

I've set out below an example of the whole process. I've taken four paragraphs – about 600 words – from an article called *Sustainable Rural Development.* (You will find it referred to in chapter 12.) I decided to make a summary of this – which is approximately 560 words long – in no more than 100 words. After the extract, you'll find the notes I made and my final summary. Here is the extract from the article:

> *What is urgently needed now are new policies that not only conserve nature but also integrate care of the Earth with care for human beings. There should be incentives to reverse the flow of people from the land to towns and cities. These people should be encouraged to do something not only worthwhile for themselves but even more worthwhile for their environments. They should be encouraged to establish communities, and build efficient and environmentally friendly homes. They should be given land to grow organic vegetables on, and they should be able to generate their own power so as to reduce their dependence on fossil fuels. These small hamlet dwellers would be able to take advantage of community farming and biomass projects. If they are well located then they could take advantage of wind, water or solar power schemes, and have little or no dependence on nationally operated utility systems. Even human waste could either be composted or put through a water reed bed purification system. Thus we would alleviate the need to be connected to the present archaic disposal system in place today.*
>
> *All that would be required to implement these ideas is a new category of land use – perhaps called Self-Sufficiency Land (SS Land). There would have to be some form of contractual agreement between the owner and the local and national authorities which would contain basic statements such as, "I will buy and live on this piece of land and will not let it out or speculate. I will conserve nature, plant over twenty trees per acre and be a co-steward in maintaining common lands. I will co-operate with my neighbours over transport, infrastructure, power generation, waste disposal, and use of available water supplies. In return for this opportunity to experience a meaningful life I will have the freedom to build my own house to a design suited to its surroundings and will also incorporate the highest energy efficient standards possible. ..."*

The consequences of implementing even small changes to current planning law to create areas of self-sufficient land would be enormous. Farmers would be able to apply for SS Land designation and if they succeeded then their land would sell for £10,000 per acre (price-capping would be necessary) instead of £1,000 per acre. Communities would then be able to set up all over the country, precipitating a marked expansion in small allied industries. Another huge benefit to the new landowners would be to receive EC grants for re-creating the woodlands and hedgerows which are at present disappearing at an alarming rate. At the same time a subsidiary income would be incurred. Apart from the cash received for planting in the first place, appropriate harvesting from the renewable resource they have planted would be materially and economically beneficial.

The boom in alternative technologies related to energy-efficient architecture and renewable energy supplies would hopefully see the beginning of the end of the Industrial Revolution and its descendants in the form of over-engineering: the kinds of engineering and technology which produce things that nobody really needs and uses up vast amounts of valuable natural resources in a very unsustainable way. Even alternative technology, as a term, is starting to have an antiquated ring about it. Perhaps a real shift in people's consciousness and sense of responsibility would be prompted by a new brand of innovators of the future: the engineers of the Environmental Revolution!

Here are my notes:
1 need policies on conservation & humans
2 Incentives needed for rural living - new communities
3 community farming/use of natural energy/environmentally-friendly sewage disposal
4 New type of land use with specific agreements between owners/ local authorities/government – Self-Sufficiency
5 Agreement: no speculative enterprises/tree planting & conservation/co-operation with neighbours on mains services. Owners able to design & build own dwellings suited to local environment
6 Results:
    (a)   farmers who applied to have their land SS designated would find it rose 10-fold in value
    (b)   explosion of new communities = expansion of small industries

(c)   landowners would get EC grants for re-creating woods & hedgerows & get profit from managing woods & selling

7 Energy-efficient building & renewable energy supplies – end of wasteful engineering & technology. All these changes cd. bring a change from industrial to environmental Rev.

Here's my draft:

Policies are needed to protect both our land and people. Incentives are needed to establish community farming and use of natural energy. There should be a newly-designated land use – Self-Sufficiency based on agreements between owners and local authorities, and government would ban land-speculation and encourage conservation and co-operation. The individual could design and build appropriate to his/her surroundings. Farmers who apply for SS designation would find their land values rose considerably in value. There would be an explosion of small industries. EC grants for creating woodlands and profit from sustainable harvesting would also benefit landowners. Wasteful engineering would end. The Industrial Revolution would give way to an Environmental Revolution.

That's 112 words. I need to lose 12.

And here's my final draft:

Policies are essential to protect land and people. Incentives are needed to establish community farming and use natural energy. A newly-designated land use – Self-Sufficiency, based on agreements between owners, local authorities and government – would ban land-speculation and promote conservation and co-operation. People could design and build appropriate to their surroundings. Farmers applying for SS designation would find land values rose. There would be an explosion of small industries. EC grants for creating woodlands and profit from sustainable harvesting would benefit landowners. Wasteful engineering would end. The Industrial Revolution would give way to an 'Environmental Revolution'.

III SUMMARIES FOR SPECIFIC PURPOSES

This can be rather more fun than basic summary-writing. You will be told to use certain material from the original to produce a piece of writing in a particular form. For this, you need to have a basic understanding of **register** and **tone** (see above).

What follows is an extract from an A-level English exam (AQA–AEB 1997). After the question and the reading material, you'll find the answer written for practice by Lorraine, a student on the course.

Test of skills of Summary Writing

The material printed on the following page is from "Small World", the newsletter of Intermediate Technology, a charity which enables impoverished communities in developing countries to use appropriate technologies for sustainable development.

Using material from the article, write an appeal leaflet for the general public, asking for funds to support the installation of micro-hydro schemes similar to the one described opposite.

Your writing must be **no longer than 200 words**, excluding any headings or sub-headings you use.

Power to the people

The dream

'People walk for miles to find out how they can get micro-hydro power. For them it is the only way they can set up a basic service in their villages and run one or two light bulbs. And for this they are prepared to invest time, labour and their tiny savings to realize a dream...'
Rafael Escobar, one of IT's local Chalan staff.

The reality

'Now that we have a mill nearby we don't have to waste hours travelling to the city; we can also improve our homes and save the money that we used to spend on candles and kerosene.'
Señora Tocas, who uses the new mill.

The highlands of Peru have an infinite number of waterfalls that could be used to generate electric power for rural areas through the establishment of small hydroelectric power plants.

Since 1989, IT Peru have established five micro-hydro plants supplying electricity to 2,000 families and a number of small businesses processing grain, milk and wood.

Micro-hydros demonstrate that small-scale local development is cost effective (in terms of quality, cost of operation and maintenance) and can be linked to other regional projects. However, further spreading of the technology and its benefits to poor communities is hampered by the lack of local finance. IT Peru is working with the Interamerican Development Bank (IDB) to offer a rotating fund through which loans can be obtained for productive projects and then repaid from profits. In addition, supportive training helps ensure viable businesses.

Energy, the motor of social development

A reliable and affordable source of energy not only saves a good deal of time and human effort, but also gives people the confidence to invest in small businesses such as workshops and mills. Surpluses may be invested in the improvement of vital community services like sanitation or poor roads. With electric lighting, children need no longer study by candle light – and their education is essential for long-term development.

The first community to benefit from this loan scheme is Chalan, an Andean village in Cajamarca district. Chalan is 50 miles as the condor flies from the national grid – a journey which takes seven hours by road.

Chalan is a village with a poor supply of drinking water, limited sanitation and only a simple health post. Basic schooling is available for children, but there is no telephone and lighting is by kerosene lamp. The things people need to improve their lives – building materials, household goods and a greater variety of foods – are not readily available, as roads and transport to the village are poor.

A community determined to help itself

What Chalan does have, however, is a community determined to help itself. Knowing better than anyone how electricity would change their lives, the village formed a committee of users and prepared and presented an application for a loan.

Every household now receiving power (about 80) contributed labour to the construction, together with people from six neighbouring villages, for it is not only Chalan which benefits.

More than 600 families will use the services of the mill or the hydro-powered battery charger which enables them to charge batteries to take home to their houses or workshops which lie outside Chalan.

Courtesy Intermediate Technology Development Group Ltd (ITDG), Bourton Hall, Bourton-on-Dunsmore, Rugby CV23 9QZ.

Effective Electric Energy Gives Power to Poor People

Your donation can give the gift of light.

How? *By generating electricity from waterfalls using small hydro-electric plants.*

Who to and where? *The people in small rural villages in Peru – miles away from the national grid.*

What will they gain? *Social development – a reliable, affordable source of energy. Basic power to all homes. More efficient work-shops and businesses. Sanitation and road building to get surplus investment. Improved schools.*

When will they get it? *Over 75 homes already supplied in small Andean village near Chalan. As many as 600 families make use of the mill or hydro-battery charger set up there.*

Who organizes all this? *IT Peru working with the Interamerican Development Bank. Loaning money for projects from a rotating fund, repaid from profits. Supportive training supplied for viable businesses.*

How can I help? *The generosity of a donation from you will help these determined people to change their lives. Their skills and your money will develop and sustain their local economy. Your kindness can give a child the chance to read by the light of a bulb instead of a candle.*

Phone: 01873 – 228866 *To pledge your donation.*

Thank you

You can see that Lorraine has adapted the material very well for the new purpose – an appeal leaflet. She has also thought very carefully about how readers might react. Note that the question states that this leaflet is for the *general public*. So it was important to omit jargon and to use simple explanations.

By constructing a series of questions to use as headings, Lorraine can focus a reader's mind on just the points that she wants to put across; in fact, she skilfully leads a reader through the information, giving examples that are likely to affect the emotions, and ending on a plea for money.

This is exactly what was needed. The purpose of the leaflet is to raise funds. So Lorraine must tug at people's heartstrings while assuring them that these projects are above board and successful. Her decision to end on a child's *chance to read by the light of a bulb instead of a candle* is just right: readers are left with that image immediately before being asked for money.

It was important to give an impression of professionalism through careful layout and use of language. Notice that Lorraine gives plenty of factual information but that she keeps it brief. Look, however, at her use of emotive language: *the gift of light, help, generosity,* and *kindness.* These words will all help to sway a reader's emotions.

My only serious criticism of this piece of work is the omission of verbs. Lorraine has concentrated so hard on getting the layout, language and tone right that she's forgotten to check that each sentence has a working verb. When items are set out in bullet points, like my list above in the section 'Writing instructions', working verbs are unnecessary. But whenever you write along the line using sentences with full stops, working verbs are *essential.*

Sometimes, an exam question will actually ask you to write notes. This means that you will be expected to include things like lists, bullet points, abbreviations, and dashes. In that situation, you would be penalized for writing full sentences containing working verbs.

SUMMARY

This chapter has covered:

- definitions of style
- simplicity
- writing instructions
- describing a process
- tone
- persuasive writing
- register
- basic summary-writing
- summaries for specific purposes

Note: Hints on answering the above question are the responsibility of the author and have not been provided by AQA.

10 Creative writing

INTRODUCTION

Many courses for mature students now include a section on creative writing. There are a number of reasons for this. It's now widely acknowledged that developing the imagination is important for developing the intellect. It has also been found that practice in structuring a piece of creative work is valuable groundwork for structuring essays and other assignments. So you may be asked to do some autobiographical work or to write a poem or story.

Autobiographical work is not set because the tutors want to pry into students' past lives. It has been found that taking a serious look at certain aspects of our past gives us a very good foundation for further study. I'd like to reassure you at once that private issues that you want to keep private can stay that way. There will be plenty left that you are quite happy to write about, and you are likely to be given a pretty free hand over what you decide to work on.

Have you ever wondered why most of us were asked to write poems at school? It's easy to think of poetry-writing as a way of keeping children quiet for half an hour, but there are more important reasons than this for having poetry on the curriculum. Writing a poem on an event, scene, or something about which we feel strongly forces our brains to perform new tricks. Just as with autobiographical work, our writing skills and imagination come into play, but in slightly different ways.

One of the reasons for asking you to write a short story is that you'll be working on structure. You will need to spend time thinking how to introduce your characters and get them interacting (the beginning), you will need to keep the plot going throughout the story (the middle), and you'll have to bring everything to a believable conclusion, with all the loose ends neatly tied up (the end). This is all very valuable practice for essay-writing and for logical thinking.

I AUTOBIOGRAPHICAL WRITING

As I explained above, if you have to write an autobiographical project, no one will be wanting you to reveal things that you want to keep private. You may be asked to concentrate on educational issues, but you are bound to have a degree of choice, and you will almost certainly be encouraged to broaden your account to include various memories. There are sure to be a some items in the following list that you'd be comfortable with:

▶ Ideas for autobiographical writing

pre-school education
evening classes
Sunday School
games
life-changing events
secondary school
places you visited
sports
grandparents
rules and regulations
furniture
religious observation
birthdays and anniversaries
having children
ornaments
brothers and sisters
marriage
festivals/rituals
the 1970s (or other decade)
popular music

school trips
clothing
museums and galleries
money
primary school
hobbies
Christmases
transport
father
jobs
hospital, doctors and health
wearing uniform
toys
household items and gadgets
clubs and societies
mother
wider family
national events
politics

Autobiographical work is particularly good for forcing us to consider the differences between a personal (and often emotional) response to people and events and a more logical, detached approach. As a serious student, you need to be able to differentiate clearly between the emotional and the logical. You need to be able to spot attempts – in what you hear and read – to manipulate your emotions; and you need to be able to think and write logically.

This is not to say that you are expected to have no emotions. The idea is to learn to be *aware* of emotion in both ourselves and others and to be able to stand back and present facts and opinions in a balanced manner. For autobiographical work, you will almost certainly be asked to tell it how it was, and then to reflect on what happened and add some comment. If you have painful memories, this kind of exercise can sometimes be a way to exorcise things and to put them in perspective. It's often by revisiting the past that we can prepare for the future.

Writing autobiography can also develop our skills with language and our use of imagination. In order to write about the past, we need to recall – and probably visualize – scenes and events. In transferring these memories to a written account, we have to use our powers of imagination by selecting and describing what we record. As we struggle to do this, we are getting wonderful practice in developing our skills with language. The process of imagining has been found to be a crucial part of developing our brains. It helps us to deal with incoming information in new ways, and can make it easier for us to cope with the workload of academic courses. If you have time to do some really serious work on your autobiography, you are likely to find that it is an extremely worthwhile and rewarding exercise.

There is one area that your tutors may be particularly keen for you to explore, and that is your educational experience. They won't want to know about failures and expulsion from school (unless you want to focus on harsh things), but they may well want you to look at:

- what you were taught (or not)
- how classes were organized
- what the buildings were like
- what types of school you attended
- what the staff were like
- what you enjoyed/hated.

They'll want to know how these things affected you at the time and how you view them in retrospect and in relation to what you now know of the rest of society. So you can see that *both* emotion and logic are vital here. It can also be very illuminating to relate our own experiences to the national situation or even to international events.

▶ Digging into your memory

You may now be thinking, "Well, OK, I'm not totally against doing this, but I just can't remember anything." If so, I sympathize. There are ways, however, of overcoming this kind of mental block. Try a small experiment now. Look at the lists below and, without stopping to think too hard, pick any item, take a sheet of notepaper, and, before reading any further, quickly do a mind map on it. (For an explanation of mind-mapping, see chapter 6.)

teachers	sports	art	money
meals	lessons	music	discipline
friends	buildings	drama	school meals
prefects	prizes	poetry	uniform
books	pictures	break times	festivals

A slightly different way of getting yourself started is to construct a life-line. For this you will probably need several sheets of A4 paper laid end to end on their sides and taped together. Part of a roll of wallpaper would also work; but if you use this, you may need to write on it with a soft crayon rather than a pen or pencil in order to avoid tearing it.

At the left-hand side, put the date you were born, and on the right put 'NOW'. Mark the whole sheet off in decades, and then begin to fill in key dates: starting school, moving house, starting work, meeting a partner, and so on. Putting in the obvious things will cause your mind to focus more clearly. You will begin to remember things you thought you'd forgotten, and you'll also be getting an overall view of your experiences.

Another useful thing to do is to start digging out actual items that relate to your past educational experiences. You could look for:

photos	diaries	scrapbooks
school reports	cups or certificates	newspaper cuttings
badges	letters	exercise books

Then you might start talking to relatives and friends, asking them specific questions and encouraging them to dip into their own memories for you. If you live near one of your old schools, you might visit it. If it's in another part of the country, you could write to the head teacher. There are likely to be photos and pamphlets that you could get copies of. There's always material available somewhere. If your old school has been razed to the ground, there are still likely to be records in the local Education Department and reference library.

Once you get going on this project, you are more likely to be swamped with material than to be short of it, and your problem will not be wondering what to write but deciding what to omit.

▶ Primary and secondary sources

You may be beginning to see that autobiographical work develops more than your literary skills. It's inevitable that you will be doing work related to both sociology and history. For example, in historical terms, all those photos, diaries and school badges from the past have a special name. They are called **primary sources**. These are things that originated in the period you are looking at. Any school records you can manage to get hold of are also primary sources. If you were really keen, you could also go and look at Education Acts and other legal documents. All these are primary sources too.

A **secondary source** looks at what happened and comments on it. This is what historians do all the time, and it's what you will be doing too. A secondary source is usually written some time *after* events take place. You may, however, come across some secondary sources that were written during the period you are looking back at. For example, let's suppose that you went to primary school in the 1960s. A textbook written in the 1960s on how geography was being taught to primary children at that time would be a secondary source. If, however, you still possess a school project on your local town or village that you put together in the 1960s, you have a primary source.

Once you begin to relate your own experiences to the experiences of others and to national events, your work will become more and more interesting. What you write will, inevitably, depend on the structure or title you've been given by your tutor; but whatever you do, you are bound to end up with a valuable perspective on certain issues from the past.

▶ Structuring your autobiographical project

The important thing here is to have a plan (see chapter 6). It's very easy to get so immersed in reminiscences that you end up forgetting the reason for doing this piece of work. Your tutor will almost certainly give you very clear guidelines. If not, do ask for information on exactly what is wanted.

You might refer to events chronologically, or you might section your material by topic. If you make a good plan, you will be able to keep focused and prevent yourself from putting in information that's not related to the assignment you've been set.

It's a good idea to include:

- clear descriptions
- a logical structure
- reflection on the past from where you stand now
- some reference to local, national or international events.

II POETRY

If you were asked to write an account of a particular poem in prose, you would probably find yourself writing something quite a lot longer than the original poem. We can say that poets nearly always *condense* what they want to tell us. So if you've been asked to write a poem, one of the things you'll be practising is the art of getting your ideas across in a few words.

You probably know the old saying that a picture is worth a thousand words. Well, poems very often contain a lot of pictures – or **images**. The poet uses his or her imagination to come up with images that will spark a reader's imagination and so help that reader to understand what the poet is thinking and feeling. As I said above, it has been found that using the imagination is a very valuable activity for developing brainpower. A brain that is used only for facts and figures is likely to function less well than one that is also used for making new and unusual connections between different topics and ideas. You may have noticed that some of your best ideas for assignments seem to come to you 'out of the blue'. This is just one example of your brain working in an apparently non-logical fashion.

One of the best ways to get yourself going on writing poems is to read some poetry. You might get a couple of books out of the library. Don't try to read them from cover to cover. Just flick through and read whatever takes your fancy. Or you might pop into a large bookshop where you can browse for ages without being pressured to buy anything.

It is sometimes thought that poetry comes wholly from the imagination, but this is rarely the case. A good poem is usually rooted firmly in facts. Notice how, in the following poem, almost all the emotion is evoked through the choice of the items that are included:

A Sunny Day in February

Going to your funeral, I noticed:

the black border on a road sign

early daffodils, growing in bunches

a name: The Bridge Café

trees frothing blossom, baby-fresh pink and white

'Mother's Day' chalked red across a board.

Finally, I saw blooms in autumn shades

arranged according to the custom.

Charles Anketell-Jones, b. 25.5.55, d. 17.2.98.

Poems are as different as the people who write them, and they can be on any topic under the sun. So don't feel that your poems have to conform to some set structure. As the writer, you can structure your poem in whatever way you feel gets the sense across best.

I'd suggest that you give yourself two rules: no rhyme and no humour. Writing good rhyme is a skill that can be hard to learn, but writing poor rhyme is relatively easy. If you go for rhyme at this stage, what is likely to happen is that you will do it at the expense of thought and emotion. It is fatally easy to focus on finding a rhyme for a word you've just written, and consequently to lose track of overall meaning. Humour can function in a similar way. The joke becomes more important than the meaning of the poem.

It would be a good idea now to choose a scene that you'd like to use for writing a poem. It needs to be somewhere that you can go and have a look at before you start to write. You might want to have a broad picture: a park, a townscape, a beach, a railway station, a mountain view or a market. On the other hand, you might like to go for a smaller picture: one building, or a single flower-bed, perhaps. The only important thing is that you need to be really interested in this place. You will write more convincingly about a junkyard than a palace if you are fascinated by junk.

When you get a moment, go to this place with a notebook and spend some time jotting down notes on whatever you find there. You are going to practise clear recording of your observations; this skill is crucial whatever you are studying. You will need to focus on things like shapes, colours, textures, light, sound, and movement. If there are people around, you'll need to look at their clothing and body language. Maybe one or two people stand out. Your task is to provide yourself with plenty of data.

When you go home and begin to write, you will need to have enough facts to choose from in order to make your poem truthful and precise. You'll see from the student poem below that it's also possible to use this technique in a poem that relies on your memories of the past. For that, you will need a really good memory and the ability to look at your past experiences with a fresh eye.

When you come to start writing your poem, try to make sure that you won't be disturbed. The imagination doesn't take kindly to being interrupted, so you may need to wait until everyone has gone to bed. Alternatively, you may find that getting up early is the answer. Start by looking through your notes. You will not want to use everything you have written down. If you did that, the resulting poem would sound more like a police report of a crime scene. Pick out things that especially interest you or that seem in some way to portray the atmosphere of the scene, and, at this stage, allow your feelings to be fully involved.

The next stage is a little bit magical. Just sit quietly, mull over your notes, reimagine the scene, and then see what turns up. What goes on in the brain at this point is something about which we know little and certainly have very little control. You may like to close your eyes; you may like to stare out of the window. You may then find that two or three quite separate phrases occur to you. You may find that you start to describe one particular item. Whatever comes, write it down straight away. If by any chance you are stuck, start to describe something anyway, using your notes to help you. But don't worry if your work looks very disjointed at this stage. The imagination likes freedom to play.

It's a good idea to aim to write a poem of between twelve and twenty lines. You can arrange it in from three to five verses (or **stanzas**). This will give you enough space to create a strong picture while still making sure that you condense your ideas. When you have written as much as you can, put the whole thing away for a day or so. You may very well find that other ideas now start to suggest themselves – usually at very inconvenient times. So if you can have a jotter handy wherever you go, you'll be able to record ideas that would otherwise almost certainly be lost. My first poem began unannounced while I was cleaning the bathroom!

The final stage is editing, and for this you need to use all your knowledge of grammar and punctuation to make the poem sharp and easily understood. One of the myths about poetry is that you can put anything down and that you don't have to write fully-functioning sentences. Only serious poets can get away with this kind of thing, and when they do it they do it for particular reasons. They are unlikely to do it very often. The process of editing can be tricky, but it's all part of the fun, and it will do wonders for your language skills.

Here's an example of a student poem. It's followed by the first draft (there were others too) and the background notes that were made before starting on the poem itself. Along the way, I've added some comment.

The Solitary Summer

Excitement and anxiety gripped me,
"Just five turns in the lane and we'll be there."
Nature itself appeared to herald us, the flowers
swaying in the breeze like hands waving, the summer sun
bright and the sky as enticing as the sea on a hot day.
– Only I saw clouds on the horizon.

They waited to greet us as we arrived.
Him, imposing but smiling, and her, ever ready with hugs for all.
The cottage, like a scene from a picture postcard,
was before us. Its stout wooden door was
framed by honeysuckle, whose aromatic scent,
although admired by the others, invaded my nostrils.

Then they were gone, and we three were left,
to be looked after and loved by those, not our parents.
"They're together, that's the main thing," I'd heard them say,
but the three of us weren't together, only two,

and all I saw of them were their backs,
as we biked, climbed, or picnicked, "together".

Their time was spent on exciting adventures.
While mine was spent with she who hugged.
Our place was the kitchen all homely and warm, with its big
wooden table, and shelf upon shelf of herbs, spices, pickles, and
jams, and the big miracle milk pan which changed milk to cream.
There, without the two, I was happy, contented.

Have a look back at the imagery in this poem. It focuses on the natural
world and on items in the kitchen. Here, the writer seems to have given
a straight list in order to create atmosphere, but we can see from her
notes that she chose carefully what to include.

First draft

Summer on the Farm

Just five turns in the lane and we'll be there,
Excitement and worry gripped me.
The blue sky had a few dark clouds on the horizon,
All we saw seemed to welcome us/the bright summer sun
The flowers waved their heads as hands saying hello
– flowers waving their heads as hands saying hello
The smell of fresh bread and cooking apples
filled the air of the old farmhouse.

Simba yelped and danced around us in delight
Big smiles from him and big hugs from her
The kitchen, its big wooden table,
shelves of herbs and spices.
Its big miracle milk pan which turned milk to cream,

the clear blue sky,
– only I saw those grey clouds on the horizon.

The almost clear blue sky except for the
hint of something threatening.

And now, luxury flats and an old people's home
remain – and memories.

Background notes

<u>smells</u>	<u>sounds</u>
bread, apples, stewing, baking	birds, cows, horses
mothballs, summer	tractors, Simba barking
cow dung, cut grass/hedges	TV, bees in long grass meadow
lily of the valley	G & Gdad talking, cockerel
	P & S laughing

<u>inside sights</u>	<u>outside sights</u>
big wooden table	large trees towering over me
high beds in my room	gates, fields
large silvery milk pan	barns, animals, tractors
row upon row of jam jars full	backs of P & S in distance
of jam, pickles & marmalade	chickens

<u>feelings being there</u>
love for Gran
adventure, being on holiday
loneliness, spending much time on my own
missing home & parents
dislike for P & S for always leaving me

In this poem, the pain of the writer's isolation from her siblings is contrasted with the beauty of their surroundings at the grandparents' home. The reason for the trip is not made clear, and it hovers with some menace in the background in the words

"They're together, that's the main thing,"

We realize from this that there has been a crisis. The fact that the writer doesn't say exactly what it was actually makes the poem stronger.

III SHORT STORIES

If you are on an Access to Higher Education course, you could well be asked to write at least one story. Adults often respond to this demand with shock horror, saying that they've not written a story since they were at school. You can view it quite differently, however, by saying, "Well, if I could do this at the age of eight, I'll be able to do it a lot better now." Your experience of life and, particularly, of people, is vast compared to that of an eight-year-old.

Character work will develop your skills of understanding and analysis, and writing the story will develop your language skills. Since imagination is crucial for each stage, you'll be developing that too, and if you've read the section on writing poems, you already know how valuable the imagination is. So if you are feeling at all negative about this process, you might remind yourself how much can be gained from it.

▶ Choosing your theme

You might start by recalling stories you've read and considering which ones you've especially liked. Why do certain things grab you? Is it because a plot is well constructed? Or perhaps you are fascinated by certain characters and by how people act and react. Or maybe you love good, sharp descriptions. You may be drawn to a particular type (**genre**) of fiction – historical, crime, or adventure, perhaps. Think for a minute about what you've really enjoyed.

Your tutor will be looking for a good structure (beginning, middle and end), believable characters, descriptions that make the story come alive, and language that fits your particular topic and situation. You need to focus, therefore, on providing these things. That will probably mean steering clear of the following: autobiography, epics that go well over the word-limit you've been given, personal hobby-horses, politics, sex and/or violence, horror, humour, science fiction and dreams (which are usually the ultimate cop-out).

Now you are probably wondering if there's anything left. In a nutshell, what you want is some interaction between two or three people, at least one of whom is changed – at least in some small way – by the events that you recount. It's especially important to create believable characters and a good structure for your story if you decide to write in any of those categories mentioned above.

The crux of a good short story is **conflict**. Readers are interested in problems and difficulties. You don't need civil strife, but you do need to show human beings struggling with some kind of difficult situation. One of the best student stories I ever read was about a tramp living rough in a local park. A teenage girl tries, briefly, to offer him some kindness, and her boyfriend turns nasty about it. That's all. But I've always remembered this story for its sensitivity.

There was a very touching moment when the poor man sniffed some flowers, saying, "Luvly cullus." He meant, of course, "Lovely colours", and the spelling beautifully creates the sound of his voice. The fact that he could take pleasure in scent and colour, even though his life involved great hardship, showed that there was far more to him than to the loutish boy who objected to his girlfriend showing kindness to someone who hadn't managed to make a success of his life. The story told, very simply, what the tramp and the girl thought and felt. It also included some good descriptions of the park, and some brief snatches of conversation. It ended with the boy practically dragging his girl-friend from the scene.

▶ Plot

If you think back to any good story you've read, you'll realize that there must be an awful lot left out. If a guy goes shark fishing, for example, we don't want to know that on the previous day he washed his socks, sent his aunt a birthday card and had a bit of indigestion. What you need are key items that will demonstrate character and advance the plot. If your man is to encounter danger, you can begin to indicate what's likely to happen by showing him preparing his boat. He may be meticulous; he may be negligent.

In a short story, your plot needs to be very simple. Here's an example:

1 A loves B
   A helps B with various difficulties
   B meets C and falls in love
   A is desolate

Here's another:

2 The Smiths move to a new home
   Mrs Smith hates the area
   They argue and problems in the marriage are revealed
   They separate/are reconciled/fight/go into counselling/what
      ever you like

And here are about a hundred and twenty-five others:

3 A wants to change jobs
buy a particular home/car
emigrate
save
spend
etc., etc.

A is blocked by B
lack of money
health
B & C
age
time
etc., etc.

The outcome is that A wins through
finds a new way
commits suicide
enlists the help of D
accepts the situation
cheers up
gets angry
etc., etc.

Here are some tips on how to cope with the above outlines:

1 Here you could keep the story short by merely *referring* to some of the difficulties encountered. You would need to relate only one in any detail. Likewise, you'd need to show only one key point in the relationship between B and C for readers to cotton on.

2 It's not necessary to describe the move. You could refer to it neatly in one sentence:

Three months after the move, the Smiths' hall was still blocked with boxes.

Then you need one argument followed by a move towards the final outcome. You don't need to accompany the couple the whole way to their changed existence.

3 Here you can, I hope, begin to see the infinite possibilities. You can take any one person and put him or her in whatever situation you like – as long as it's believable. Chose just the key points in the episode you want to cover, add some description, a snatch or two of conversation, and you've created a human drama.

Each of these plots is clear and well defined. In each case, you could focus on two or three situations that would encapsulate the whole story. Go for highlights rather than a moment-by-moment account.

▶ Writing about what you know

This is valuable advice that is given to all new writers. If you were writing about the Smiths and their marriage problems, stick to describing the kind of people and living quarters that you have personal experience of. You will be convincing on what you know about – whether it's poverty, dog-racing or the Women's Institute.

▶ Descriptions

If you've worked through the section on poetry, you know what to do here. If your story is set in the local bus station, pop along there and make some notes. You might get something like this:

yellowing paint – peeling near seats
concrete – hard, cold
queues/crush of people
lines of bus stops/buses – red & white/coaches
wind
café – plastic cups
information boards – small print
inspector – peaked cap – holding small board
sound – voices/brakes/engines running
child in pushchair – asleep
smell of diesel

You may only use two or three items from your list when you come to write, but having plenty to choose from makes things much easier, and becoming fully aware of the place will ultimately give strength to your writing. A good way of adding description to your story is to slip some in every now and then rather than adding a whole chunk in one go. Your story might be about a couple who were once lovers and who meet by chance, after many years, while changing buses on long-distance journeys. Notice which items from the above list I've used in an opening paragraph for this story:

> *The wind seemed to be blowing all the way from the Russian*
> *Steppes. Pete held the plastic cup close to his chest, warming his*
> *fingers on the heat from the hot coffee. Suddenly he saw her – or*
> *thought he did. He caught sight of the auburn hair and the angular*
> *stance. Then a crush of people surging forward to the London*
> *coach got in the way. He grabbed his holdall and started round the*
> *back of the queue in a rush, slopped coffee burning his skin.*

As you see, I've begun to show what the bus station is like without having to write a paragraph of description which would slow things down. It's cold, windy and busy. Incidentally, bus and train stations are very useful places for setting stories ·because people are there for just short periods and their emotions are often heightened as they meet, say goodbye or have arguments in the stresses and strains of travelling. There's also plenty to describe, such as cafés, news-stands, vehicles, architecture, other travellers, and so on.

► Characterization

If you need a couple of characters and you've got a mental block, you can try the local bus station. Or go into a pub or restaurant where you can sit and watch people unobtrusively. Alternatively, just go for a walk to your local shops. People are everywhere.

You will need some descriptions of clothes, expressions, movement, and so on. Make a list, just as I did for the bus station. Then use individual items from this list at relevant points. If I want to describe a young woman begging in the London Underground, I might note:

> bedraggled hair
> old brown wool coat that hangs loosely – like a sack
> trousers tucked into very worn black boots

thin dog on a blanket
knitted hat – rainbow colours
thin fingers
pallid skin
hunched sitting position

I might decide to write a story about a successful civil servant who travels daily on the Underground and is offended by the sight of beggars. The story could show how one day his viewpoint shifts. I could begin like this:

Martin's daily journey on the Tube was brief: just one stop from King's Cross to Russell Square. He rose early, parked his car in the Home Counties, read The Times *in First-Class peace on the train, braved the Tube, and took a cab at Russell Square if it was raining. He was in the habit of keeping his mind on pleasant thoughts while travelling. He often smiled at the Underground's occasional beggars to demonstrate to them that a better world lay within reach if only they would open their eyes to it.*

Why he looked more closely at Carla he was never quite sure. Maybe the bright rainbow colours of her knitted hat reminded him of his younger sister in childhood. Perhaps it was those blue eyes staring from the pallid face like a saint in a Renaissance painting. Or maybe the long, slim fingers that stroked the half-starved dog made him think of his mother. Whatever it was that had arrested him, Martin's defences had been breached.

Carla had learnt to spot indecision. Her voice was thin but her stare acted on Martin like a tap on the shoulder from the Almighty. Without shifting from her hunched position, she asked,

"Spare something for a hot meal, sir?"

You can see again that I've not given a straight description, but have started to weave items from my list into the plot as it moves along. I will need only the briefest snatches of conversation to make the characters come alive. Readers automatically start to form their own pictures from the clues they pick up.

▶ Speech

In creative writing, we can develop character through speech to build up a picture of an individual for whoever reads our work. We have to make a character sound 'real'. So we need to choose speech that is appropriate for the *type* of person who is speaking and for the *situation* in which we have put him or her.

There are two key points to writing dialogue in a short story:

1 Make it real. Real people don't speak in carefully thought-out sentences.
2 Give only the important bits.

What you want is to get the *feel* of your character on the page. The following examples will explain what I mean:

(a) *"I've had enough. I can't stand it. I'm going."*

This is a character in some kind of difficulty. Notice how the short sentences demonstrate frustration followed by decision. The repetition of *I* puts the focus on the view from one person's angle.

(b) *"Puss, puss, puss. Who's a lovely pussy-cat, then?"*

Here is the language often used to a pet. It's gentle and very simple. If your story is about a lonely person, you might underline the loneliness by demonstrating love for an animal. If those were the only words your character spoke in the whole story, this could demonstrate how he or she is cut off from society.

(c) *"Where's Darren?"*
     "He had to go early. He sees his mother Sundays."

In this story by a student, we see a girl trying to cover up the real reason her boyfriend has departed. Look carefully at the wording. If the writer had been aiming to write grammatically, that last sentence would be likely to read,

"He always sees his mother on Sundays."

In each case, above, just the key points in conversation are used. You seldom need to write much speech. You just need enough to give a flavour of a character and to heighten the reader's awareness of tensions in a particular situation.

It's worth remembering that few of us speak in carefully formed grammatical sentences, and we tend to say "Um" and "Er" rather a lot. Listen to people shopping, or having an argument, or talking on the phone. We all use gesture and stress to help get our meaning across, and we break off lots of our sentences in mid-air.

Who says what

There's nothing worse than an account which keeps repeating *he said* or *she said*. In a story in which you have two speakers in dialogue, that kind of boring repetition can be avoided rather subtly, as you will see in the exchange between Jim and Dick below:

> "Give me the loot, Jim." Dick held out his hand.
> "What for?"
> "Just hand it over and I'll stash it away." It was getting late, and Dick was beginning to get angry.
> "I'm not sure," said Jim slowly, "that I like the arrangements."
> "You flippin' idiot! Either we stash it or we're done for!"

The words *Dick held out his hand*, in the brief exchange above, let the reader know, without using that worn-out old phrase, *he said*, that it is Dick who is speaking. It's obvious, since he spoke to Jim, that it is Jim who replies. So I didn't need to put *said Jim*. Another comment on Dick's behaviour – that he was getting *angry* – again shows clearly who is speaking. Then the words *said Jim* that follow Jim's comment on being *not sure* are made more interesting by the addition of the word *slowly*, and, because of the build-up, it's clear that it is Dick who loses his temper in the end.

Another useful way of steering clear of repetition and keeping your reader awake is to use words that are more specific than *said*. In certain circumstances, you might find something that fits just right from the following list:

replied
shouted
whispered
giggled
moaned

snorted
spat
cooed

You can find lots more. Don't overdo the variations, however. Too much change can be a bad thing. But the occasional new word can be wonderfully evocative of a particular character.

▶ The beginning

Don't spend a page recounting your characters' past lives. Remember, this is a short story, not a novel. There isn't time for long explanations. Get stuck into the action straight away. I had Peter rushing after his lost love in my first paragraph (above) and Carla accosting Martin in my third. Get the characters interacting and they'll start to reveal themselves. If there's something that you *must* explain, do it as the plot moves along – as I did with my descriptions of the bus station and of Carla's appearance.

▶ The end

This is merely the ending of the story – not a summing-up of the characters' whole lives. What you need here is a resolution of whatever issues you've raised. That just means that a reader needs to know what has changed for at least one of your characters. In the story of Martin and Carla, this could be a new understanding for Martin and a consequent change in some of his behaviour. It's as well, in a short story, to stick to small changes. Readers are likely to find wholesale change unbelievable.

SUMMARY

This chapter has covered:

- autobiography: your memory
                  primary and secondary sources
                  planning

- poetry   using the imagination
  observation and note-making
  drafting
- short stories   theme
  plot
  description
  characterization
  speech
  beginnings
  endings.

11 Letters

INTRODUCTION

If you need to write letters for assessment or for an exam, there's no denying the fact that you need to get things right. This chapter will concentrate on the basics. It will look at the differences between formal and informal letters, at the accepted ways for setting these out in Britain, and at some of the different types of letter that you might be required to write.

One of the reasons behind giving letter-writing as an assignment – apart from making sure that people know how to set letters out correctly – is to give students practice in one of the following:

- giving or asking for information
- putting forward your ideas or opinions with clarity.

For information on the type of language to use, have a look at chapter 9. For help with structure, you can use chapter 6, part II. It's particularly important that you organise your paragraphs very clearly.

▶ Informal letters

When we write to close friends, we can do exactly as we like. We can break all the rules of grammar, draw pictures and even write letters of only one or two words if we want to:

Dear Alex

Yes!

Luv,

Chris xxx

These two people clearly know each other well, so Alex will be in no doubt over what this letter means. In fact, the shortness of the letter gives impact. So with letters to friends, just continue to be yourself and don't worry about doing things right or wrong. You may find, however, that, as your skills develop, some of your letters to friends become increasingly complex. Letters can be a literary form in their own right, as is clear from the number of books published containing collections of letters.

The term *informal letters* can be rather confusing. The letter to Alex is certainly informal, but it is definitely not what tutors and examiners want to see. In terms of your course, it's best to think of informal letters as letters that are friendly and helpful but that also adhere to the rules of grammar and letter-writing.

According to what country you live in – or even your age or the person who originally taught you – there may be certain variations in how you've learnt to set out your name, address, and so on. There is, however, a specific layout that British examiners now look for. So it makes sense, if you are studying for British exams, to use the accepted format. You will find, when you come to look at formal letters, that they just build on the informal structure.

There are four important items that you will need to include accurately in an informal letter:

- your address
- the date
- the salutation (saying *Hello*)
- the valediction (saying *Goodbye*).

If you are asked to write a letter to a friend, the layout expected is this:

YOUR ADDRESS
[line space]
DATE

Dear Bob
[line space]

```



```

[line space]

[blank box]

[line space]

[blank box]

[line space]

[blank box]

[line space]
Best wishes
[line space]
your first name (or nickname)

Note that, when writing a letter to a friend (even when it is for course-work or for an exam), your friend's address must *not* be included.

You might, however, be asked to write to someone who is not a friend but to whom you will need to write a friendly letter. For example, you could be asked to write a letter to a local celebrity, asking if he or she would agree to open a fête or give a talk. The layout of your letter would be the same as the one to a friend except for the salutation and valediction:

YOUR ADDRESS
[line space]
DATE

Dear ADDRESSEE'S TITLE AND LAST NAME
[line space]

[blank box]

[line space]

```
┌─────────────────────────────────────────┐
│                                         │
│                                         │
│                                         │
└─────────────────────────────────────────┘
```

[line space]

```
┌─────────────────────────────────────────┐
│                                         │
│                                         │
│                                         │
└─────────────────────────────────────────┘
```

[line space]

```
┌─────────────────────────────────────────┐
│                                         │
│                                         │
│                                         │
└─────────────────────────────────────────┘
```

[line space]
Yours sincerely
[line space]
Your signature (first name and surname)
[line space]
YOUR FULL NAME (in capitals if you write by hand)

There's no hard and fast rule about whether to sign using your first name in full or just an initial. When you want to be friendly you'll use your first name. You might decide that when you want to keep some distance – as in a letter of complaint – you'll use your initial(s). If you sign with an initial, however, whoever replies to you will need to guess whether you're male or female (see 'Titles', below). Most writers will guess that you're male, however. This problem is obviously more pressing if you're female.

It's vital to print your name. In real life, the person reading your letter could easily make a mistake in spelling when writing back to you if there is only your signature to go on.

It's also very important to use a capital *Y* for *Yours* and a small *s* for *sincerely*. Incidentally, notice how *sincerely* is spelt. People very often get the *es* in the wrong places. You might find this easier to remember if you note that the word *sincerely* contains the word *ere* (that's *here* without the *h*).

You might, of course, be asked to write to someone in their business capacity. In this case, the *shape* of your letter will be roughly the same as the one above, but there will be some things added – like this:

YOUR ADDRESS
[line space]
DATE

ADDRESSEE'S TITLE, INITIALS AND LAST NAME
ADDRESS
[line space]
Dear ADDRESSEE'S TITLE AND LAST NAME
[line space]

[line space]

[line space]

[line space]
Yours sincerely
[line space]
YOUR SIGNATURE
[line space]
YOUR FULL NAME (in capitals if you write by hand)

It's also important to remember that for neither of these letters do you put your name above your own address. This practice is common in some countries, and business letters in Britain nearly always have the name of the business at the top of the page, but it is not deemed to be correct for letters from private individuals. In fact, it is considered to be a mistake.

Let's suppose that you have been asked to write to a Mr J. Fleming, the manager of Fergus Electronics, to complain about a faulty computer purchased from them. You will set out your letter like this:

14 Lucius Street
Maxford
Teeshire
A4 7RP

15th February 2001

Mr J Fleming
The Manager
Fergus Electronics
Bat Lane
Wallopford
Nutshire WP14 6RF

Dear Mr Fleming

Three months ago, I took the decision to buy a new computer. I run a small translating business from my home, and increased work has meant that I need a new, up-to-date, reliable PC.

I was persuaded by your advertising both in the local press and on television to visit your premises for an analysis of my office needs. Once I was there, a salesman was adamant that he knew the make and model best suited to my work.

If you check your records, you will find that I have already had to return twice to have minor faults corrected. Now the machine is malfunctioning yet again.

You may imagine my anger. I do not feel that I should spend my time delivering faulty goods to your premises. Will you please arrange to have this PC replaced with a new one and inform me of the delivery date.

Yours sincerely

Robert Long

ROBERT LONG

Two things may have struck you here: there are no indentations – either for paragraphs or in the lines of the addresses, and there's no punctuation in the addresses. This layout has been in use for a number of years now – especially in government offices. It's the result of research to find the simplest method of setting out letters. You might like to check the layout in any official letters that you receive. If you are not used to this, you may feel it looks a little strange, but once you start to use it, you will find that it really is very convenient, and it saves a good deal of time. Just as with an essay, leave a line between all the paragraphs, as it makes a letter much easier to read as well as making it look smart.

Note that, even though he knows the name of the person he is writing to, Robert also includes the recipient's job title between the name and address. This is usual in business letters of any kind.

▶ Titles

There tends to be a bit of disagreement nowadays on what to do about your title (*Mrs*, *Mr*, and so on). If you leave it out, you may find that you don't get the right one on your reply. There are not likely to be any problems for a man with a straightforward name who generally uses the title *Mr*. If you sign yourself *John Brown*, you will get addressed as *Mr Brown*. If, however, you are a man and your name is Alex Brown, the person who writes back to you will have to guess at whether you are male or female if you omit your title. If you are the Reverend John Brown, you will not get addressed as such unless you give your title or your letter itself makes your situation obvious – that is, unless it contains such things as a reference to your parish duties.

Women may have different problems. When writing a letter to a woman whose preferred title is not known, it is usual nowadays to use *Ms*. If you sign yourself *Sally Brown*, you are likely to be addressed as either *Ms Brown* or *Mrs Brown*. Government offices will call you *Ms Brown*, which is fine if you don't want to let on whether you are married or not. You'll have the best chance of getting the title you want by using it yourself, like this:

Yours sincerely

Beth Parkes

BETH PARKES (Mrs)

Put your title *after* your name, and always put it in *brackets*.

Some people, however – and perhaps it started with the ones who cut out punctuation in addresses and stopped using indentations – are now cutting out titles altogether. You may or may not like this, but it's as well to be aware of what's going on. Leaving out your own title can give the impression that you are self-confident and not bothered over minor details. Sometimes, you will even find yourself addressed with your full name (and no title), whatever you do. I've received letters that begin:

Dear Jean Rose

▶ Differences between informal and formal letters

A formal letter is sometimes said to be one (like Robert Long's letter to the manager of Fergus Electronics) with the name and address of the recipient at the top left-hand side. More often, letters are divided into informal and formal, according to the salutation and valediction. A letter beginning *Dear Mrs Smith* would be said to be informal, and a letter to the same person beginning *Dear Madam* would be formal.

▶ Formal letters

If you have not yet read the section on informal letters, do glance at it now, as it contains a good deal of essential information on setting out all letters.

The letter to J. Fleming at Fergus Electronics begins *Dear Mr Fleming* and ends *Yours sincerely*. A classic formal letter is the one that begins either *Dear Sir* or *Dear Madam* (or *Dear Sir/ Madam*) and ends with *Yours faithfully*. We use this form of address nowadays, however, *only* when we don't know the name of the person to whom we're writing. If you know the person's name, it's essential to use it. If you don't know the name, you'll have to put *Dear Sir/ Madam*. It's OK to put *Dear Sir* by itself *only* if you happen to know for certain that the recipient of your letter is male. If you are sure it's a woman, then you can put *Dear Madam*.

As far as the valediction is concerned, all you have to do here is to remember to use a capital *Y* for *Yours* (just as you do with *Yours sincerely*) and a small *f* for faithfully. People sometimes have trouble in remembering whether to use *sincerely* or *faithfully* in any letter they write. Think of the *f*s: formal and faithful go together. Yes, it does all seem a bit fussy, but it's rather like knowing the accepted things to do at a wedding: everything goes more smoothly for you when you get it right.

One further bugbear can be knowing exactly who to write to. When you write a letter, you *must* address it to a particular person. This can be especially difficult when, for example, you need to write to a company and you don't know anyone's name or job title. When totally at a loss, I usually write to *The Manager*. So if Robert Long had not been given the name of the manager at Fergus Electronics, he would have written a formal letter, set out like this:

14 Lucius Street
Maxford
Teeshire
A4 7RP

15th February 2001

The Manager
Fergus Electronics
Bat Lane
Wallopford
Nutshire WP14 6RF

Dear Sir/Madam

Purchase of a fault-ridden computer

Three months ago, I took the decision to buy a new computer ...

Yours faithfully

Robert Long

ROBERT LONG

Notice that the subject of the letter is given here in bold type. This makes the letter look businesslike. The subject can be given like this both for letters that begin *Dear Sir/Madam* and those starting with the recipient's name. If you write a letter by hand, the subject must be underlined. Leave a line both before and after this heading.

Robert Long has not put his own title (Mr) after his name. With a name like Robert, it's pretty clear that he's male, so he would get addressed as such in a return letter. It is up to J. Fleming to reply politely. If Robert's preferred title was different – for example, *Revd* or *Dr*, he would probably use it to make things clear.

▶ Letters of complaint

Robert Long's letter is clearly a letter of complaint. If you need to write one of these, it's important to remember to control any feelings of anger. You will, however, be expected to be forceful. Robert stated the problem very clearly and demanded a replacement, but at no point was he abusive. It's OK to be gently humorous, but aiming for belly laughs will be frowned on. Robert has contented himself with injecting a little mild sarcasm into the letter's heading.

▶ Letters to the tabloids

There are not likely to be many occasions when you are asked to write something appropriate for a tabloid newspaper, as these letters are invariably very short and generally fairly simple. There is, however, some skill in getting the language and tone just right, and you might find a question asking for a tabloid letter on an A-level English paper as one part of a longer question.

In a letter of this type, you would expect to show some emotion and to use punchy, memorable phrases. Language should be fairly simple and sentences short. You would need to put across a strong viewpoint without going into a great deal of detail. If you have been asked to write a letter to a tabloid, check out the letters in a couple of dailies before submitting your work.

▶ **Letters to broadsheet newspapers**

You may well be given an assignment on writing for a broadsheet (one of the *heavy* newspapers). These letters need to have:

- formal language
- a good mix of simple and more complex sentences
- facts to prove your points
- an emotionally controlled tone
- a clear line of argument

There follows an example of how Richard, a student on an Access to Higher Education course, wrote a letter for coursework on his feelings about the Millennium Dome.

17 Gulf Street
Saltash
Cornwall
PL5 6SB

26th February '98

The Editor
The Times
1 Pennington Street
London E1 9XN

Dear Sir,

I am writing in response to all of the press reports and uproar over the Millennium Dome. Although the money needed to fund the Dome does seem rather excessive and could, in actual fact, be better used in other areas, the Dome itself will become a part of our children's heritage.

Children of this generation don't, in general, seem to have much of an idea about their heritage and the Dome will be a focus of such worldwide interest as a celebration of the year 2000 that hopefully children won't be able to help being interested in it. This interest, once generated, can be used by parents and teachers to kindle an enthusiasm in our nation's children and young people for our national heritage.

As yet it is not fully known just what will be included in the Dome, but that it presents a wonderful opportunity to bring our heritage and history alive in many exciting ways is obviously apparent. The country needs to use a centre like this to show children that they can learn in a very fun way and encourage them to see that both children and adults can learn and enjoy themselves at the same time.

This type of attitude would encourage the new thinking which the government advocates on 'lifelong learning', and this can bring nothing but good for our nation as a whole. The educational potential in the Dome is so vast that it would be almost criminal to waste it.

It would be hoped that those organisers and administrators of the Dome do not lose sight of the fact that it is for the people and the nation, and is not being built only for the purpose of lining somebody's pocket. If the entrance fees (if there have to be entrance fees) are too high, then great opportunities to educate and entertain a vast majority of the population will be missed. Just take for example the prices which the National Trust charge for admission to their properties. The numbers of people who have not witnessed these wonderfully kept examples of history – partly because of them having no activities, but mainly because of the high entry prices – is a national disgrace.

So it is imperative that Peter Mandelson and all those responsible for equipping the Dome, take the responsibility very seriously and see the great potential which they have control over for encouraging our nation's children and young people to view their heritage with pride.

Yours faithfully

Richard Thompson

RICHARD THOMPSON

Feedback

The language here is, in the main, sufficiently formal for a broadsheet newspaper, and the sentences are generally well constructed. The word *heritage* is used twice in paragraph two, and Richard does get a little emotional at times. The phrases *lining somebody's pocket* and *national disgrace* would be better cut out, and *a very fun way* is a bit too colloquial for a broadsheet paper. Richard explains his views clearly, although if he had intended to send this off to *The Times*, I'd have suggested he condense it. Those letters that are published are generally shorter than this and are all very tightly controlled. Richard's points on heritage could have been made more succinctly. However, as a piece of coursework at Access level this letter is perfectly adequate.

Practice in essay-writing is valuable for this type of assignment and will help you to write in an increasingly sophisticated manner – putting facts across succinctly and setting out strong or novel ideas in a forceful but controlled tone.

SUMMARY

This chapter has covered:

- letters to friends

  your address – on the right
  date – underneath your address
  salutation – *Dear* [Bob]
  valediction - *Best wishes*

- polite informal letters

  your address – on the right
  salutation – *Dear Mrs Jones*
  the subject of the letter underlined (if applicable)
  valediction – *Yours sincerely*
  your name in capitals underneath your signature (with your preferred title in brackets afterwards)

- formal letters

  your address – on the right
  date – underneath your address
  recipient's job title and address – on the left

salutation – *Dear Sir/ Madam*
the subject of the letter underlined
valediction – *Yours faithfully*
your name in capitals underneath your
     signature (with your preferred title in
     brackets afterwards)

- Characteristics of letters to broadsheet newspapers
  formal
  factual
  controlled
  well-argued

12 Articles

INTRODUCTION

Many educational courses nowadays require students to write one or more articles suitable for magazines. If you have not done this before, you may be feeling nervous. I hope, however, that by the time you've read this chapter, you'll realize that article-writing can be a lot of fun. You will get the most out of it if you proceed as if you intended to submit your article to a magazine.

The important thing is to make sure that you choose a topic you are interested in, and that you then throw yourself into the task with enthusiasm. Your enthusiasm will inevitably show in your finished piece and will transfer to anyone who reads it. If you follow the guidelines here, you are likely to wow your tutor with a really accomplished piece of work. You might even produce something that you really could get published.

The way you write your article will depend very much on the course you are taking and the guidelines you've been given. If you are in the early stages of an Access course, you will not be expected to go into too much depth or provide too many facts. Many Access courses are now structured in two levels – 2 and 3. If you are working on a unit at level 3, or if you are studying for A level, you will be expected to produce more sophisticated work.

If you want to write for children, do check this out with your tutor before beginning. In some cases, writing for children would be quite acceptable because doing this requires particular skills. For other assignments, however, it would be important to write for adults.

If you have not yet looked at the sections on 'Register' and 'Tone' in chapter 9, it would be a good idea to do that now.

The skills covered in this chapter are the basic requirements for any level of article-writing, but they are by no means exhaustive. If you become really interested in this type of writing, you will probably want to read more about it – and possibly go on to take a course in journalism.

If you have been given a completely free choice over what you do for your article, you may be thinking that a free magazine would be the easiest type to write for. Unless you are really pushed for time, I'd advise against this. Free magazines generally have less clear-cut policies on how they want items written, and this might make you believe that writing for a Freebie would be an easy option. It is likely, however, that writing a piece for a more upmarket magazine would be less of a struggle simply because what is wanted is generally so much clearer. Just as with essays, having a clear structure and firm boundaries makes it far less likely that a writer will waffle or produce work that doesn't fit the bill.

▶ Starting from scratch

The first thing, of course, is to make a broad decision on your topic. If you've been given a subject area, you will need to narrow this down to something quite specific. It's likely that you have been given a word-limit somewhere between one and two thousand words. That will give room for you to cover one quite small area in sufficient depth.

As with all assignments, the best thing is to start with a mind map. Let's suppose that you are studying child development and that you have been asked to write a magazine article on any aspect of development of the under-fives. Your initial mind map might look something like this:

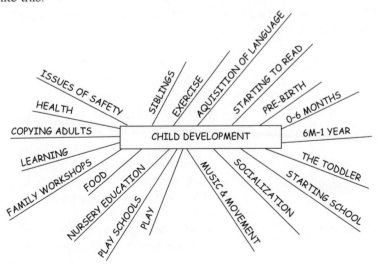

Remember that, at this stage, it's useful to throw down absolutely everything you can think of without worrying whether or not your ideas seem sensible. You might even leave this map around for a day or two so that you can add any new ideas that come to you.

From this idea-finding exercise you will choose your topic area. If I were doing this assignment, I might choose 'acquisition of language' as my topic. You may feel that you don't know enough about *any* of the areas you've come up with to write on them, but we all often feel that about any assignment or essay. It's a perfectly normal initial response to the task. Look at the topics about which you already know *something* (from lectures, reading, experience, and so on) and just choose the one you are most interested in.

▶ Choosing a magazine to write for

In order to write a good article you need to have a very clear understanding of the people you are writing for – your *target audience* – and what you hope your article will do for them. Magazine editors know their readership. They are well aware that if they publish material that doesn't interest their readers, sales will slump and they will soon be out of a job. So the material in all magazines is very carefully targeted at a specific readership (audience). When choosing your magazine, therefore, you need to spend a little time thinking about who reads it.

The following table will give you a rough sense of some of the different types of magazines published and of their readers. It's by no means an exhaustive list, but it should get you thinking.

Type of magazine	Audience
Popular	Must cater for those with limited reading ability
General	Very wide range – subject matter must be suitable for people from different social backgrounds and with varied work experience
Subject-specific	Many readers will know a great deal and will want read something new to them
Academic	Readers will expect serious material that is new, well referenced and written in a sophisticated manner

Children's general	Treatment must be lively and language simple – facts should be clear and accurate
Children's subject-specific	Facts are essential, but language must be very clear
Women's	Levels are varied; emotional and personal issues are generally important
Family	Every topic *must* relate to family issues and language must be very clear and straightforward
Coffee-table	Lightweight treatment needed, though accuracy is essential – pictures are crucial
Freebies	There is a very wide range of free magazines – many have specific subject areas, but criteria are generally much less specific than in the main press

You can be looking for a suitable magazine while you get your research under way; or you may already have a magazine in mind. If not, spend some time in newsagents and/or one of the larger libraries to see just what's around. This process need not take you long and you'll probably find it interesting. When you come across a magazine that you like – and in which you think your topic would fit – you will need to look in more detail at the kind of articles printed:

- how long are the articles?
- how much detail is included?
- what do they assume that readers already know?
- who are these readers?
- how old are they?

You can often tell a lot about the readership of a magazine from the type of adverts it carries. Clearly, expensive cars are usually bought by the well-off and/or successful. Walking gear is bought by people with an interest in the outdoors and in keeping fit.

The more you know about the readers of a particular magazine, the easier it is to decide what to include in your article. In fact, you could almost say that the readers are the most important aspect of the work.

It's essential to try to step into their shoes and work out what will keep them interested. If I were to write my article on language acquisition, the facts would remain constant whatever magazine I aimed my piece at, but the number and type of facts I included and the style and language I used would be specific to the readership of one magazine.

Anyone who wants to sell an article to a specific magazine is usually advised to look at a minimum of three back copies. This is in order to get a really clear idea of what type of article that particular magazine publishes. The current issue could be a one-off in which general policy is temporarily suspended. It might be just your luck to find an edition that celebrates some centenary from cover to cover. This would be likely to give you a false impression of the magazine. So try to look at several issues. If, however, you've chosen an expensive magazine that's published only once a quarter and is not held in your library, you may have to make do with one issue.

Researching the topic

At this stage, the work will be very similar to what you do when writing an essay: you need to find out facts, ideas and opinions. Whatever magazine you decide to angle your work towards, you will need facts. If you are working on a topic covered on your course, ask your tutor to suggest books and other material that you might look at to broaden your knowledge. After all, this assignment will have been designed as a way for students to extend their knowledge and understanding. If that doesn't yield anything, ask a librarian to point you in the right direction. Getting hold of material for an article can actually be more fun than researching for an essay, because you have more of a free hand. Here's a selection of items that may prove useful:

- academic books and journals
- magazines – especially those catering for special interests
- maps
- encyclopaedias
- tapes/videos/CDs
- minutes of Local Authority proceedings
- publications by societies
- journals of statistics
- autobiographies and letters.

Getting the facts right for an article is of crucial importance. Magazines have a wide circulation. Anyone who publishes incorrect material is likely to find that subsequent issues of the magazine carry irate letters pointing out errors in gruesome detail. So work as if you were doing this for real.

Interviews

Talking to someone involved in the field you are writing about can be a real eye-opener and can provide very valuable material for your article. A quote from the horse's mouth can add strength to your own explanations.

So where do you find a willing victim? There may be someone in a local college or university who works in the field you are covering. The main switchboard of the college will put you through. Another way of locating people is through *Yellow Pages*. There are thousands of different companies and other organizations listed here. Your reference librarian might suggest local societies that you could contact. Once you begin, one link often leads to another.

All you have to do is ring up, explain that you have to write an article for an assignment, mention the subject matter, and ask if your quarry could spare you fifteen minutes face-to-face. If the person refuses, thank them and go on to someone else. You may be told that you will have to conduct your interview on the phone. If this happens, you'll be glad if you've already prepared your questions.

Always take a prepared question sheet to an interview. It's a good idea to set out your page something like the one below so that it's really easy to take notes:

INTERVIEW: *(subject's name)*

1 What areas of *a* do you cover?

2 What is your specific interest?

3 How often does *b* happen?

4 What is your view on *c*?

5 Can you explain *d* for me?

6 Can you suggest where I might find out more about *e*?

Preparing a question sheet will help to get your mind in gear, so it's very useful preparation even if the interview takes a completely different turn. Sometimes, an interviewee may not be happy to see things being written down. If that is the case, you will need to find somewhere to write as soon as you leave. If you wait till you get home, key facts can be forgotten.

When you write up your article, you will need to show clearly what information you received from this particular source. If you want to give an exact quote of something that was said, follow the rules for setting out **direct speech** in chapter 5.

You can also quote key figures from the field. The American academic, Steven Pinker, who writes on language, is sometimes seen on British TV. If I noted down one or two things he said, they would look good in my article on language acquisition.

▶ Angling your topic to your chosen magazine

If I were to write that article on language acquisition, I would need to look very carefully at the level of complexity required by the magazine I had chosen. I'd do this before writing a single word.

If I wanted to write for a general or weekly women's magazine, I'd need to put a limit on the number of facts I mentioned, keep analysis quite short, and either steer clear of jargon or make quite sure that I gave explanations for any technical terms. Here, I'd need to give examples from everyday life. Many magazines use the trick of relating issues directly to individual people in order to get complex issues across (see under 'Human interest', below).

If I were to write the article for children, I'd make sure that my language was simple and that my explanations were especially clear. People sometimes think that it must be really easy to write for children. Don't be fooled. Writing something really clear and simple that is still interesting is not a walkover. Do check with your tutor, however, that writing a piece for children will be acceptable for your assignment.

If I wanted to write an article suitable for a nursing magazine, facts would be crucial (as in an academic article), but any analysis would need to be really clear. I would also need to relate my comments directly to a nurse's experience of children within a hospital setting, so I'd probably need to talk to one or two nurses. Readers of a nursing magazine would soon spot errors. Remember, when writing for members of a particular profession or people with knowledge of a specific subject area, you need to think about what they already know and also give them something that will be new to them.

If I'd read a good deal and I'd been doing really well, and if I knew from tutor feedback that my ideas on this aspect of the course were lively and interesting, I might decide to aim my article at an academic journal. In this case, the article might look rather similar to my essays. I'd need to pay special attention to careful referencing of any quotations and factual evidence. (See chapter 7.)

Once you've got your material together and decided on a magazine, it's time to make a rough plan. I say 'rough' because, until you actually submit your article, you need to be prepared to make many amendments. Drafting is a vital part of the process. So make what we can call a working plan just to get yourself going. (See the section 'The plan' in chapter 6.) Now you can begin to write.

▶ Openings

As with essays, it's often best to leave the actual writing of your opening paragraph(s) until last. This is because (a) you may not know how to introduce your article when you're not yet sure exactly what you're going to say and (b) you may be terrified and unable to start anyway. So leave the opening and start in the middle if that feels more comfortable. The main thing is to begin somewhere.

When you are ready to write your opening, the following examples may give you some ideas. Each writer presents an interesting idea right at the start in a bid to 'hook' readers who are likely to turn over and read something else if their appetites are not whetted immediately. The aim is to grab your readers by the throat and hang on to them.

The first piece is from a magazine called *Devon Life*. It's aimed particularly at the tourist trade and so it's geared to attracting people to the county of Devon in south-west England. The title of the article is 'Plymouth City Centre'. Notice how Bob Mann, the author, opens on a mildly controversial note and so aims to 'hook' both those who will like the city and those who might at first be less enthusiastic:

> The heart of post-war Plymouth is a grid pattern of wide, traffic-free streets, which some people find inspiringly open and expansive, and others find confusing and over-exposed to the weather.

Anybody reading this is likely to begin wondering how they themselves will feel about this city – and at that point the writer has them 'hooked'.

My next example is from *The Countryman*. This is a magazine whose readers like to look at country life from a traditional angle. They want to read about nature, country crafts, history, and country people. Ian Mitchell has written an article about a woman who, at the turn of the twentieth century, managed to make ends meet by offering refreshments and bed-and-breakfast accommodation in her crofter's cottage in Scotland. Note that Mitchell's first ploy to 'hook' the reader is to do spot of name-dropping. He then goes straight for the stomach:

> When William Gladstone, as prime minister, used to have to stay at Queen Victoria's summer residence, Balmoral, he found relief from attendance on a less than congenial monarch through strenuous hikes over the Cairngorms. On his way back to official duty, he would find sustenance at Thistle Cottage, Inverey, purchasing there a bag of Mrs Gruer's scones.

The extract below is from an article by Mark, a student who had looked very carefully at how writers begin articles with that 'hook' for a specific readership. His article is called 'Sustainable Rural Development' and is aimed at *Resurgence*, a magazine that covers environmental issues, alternative lifestyles and New Age theories and ideas. He hits just the right note by referring to Arthurian legend:

> *Vortigern the Tyrant wanted to build a Great Tower, but every time he tried the tower fell down. Even his wisest counsellors were unable to tell him what was wrong. Then Merlin was brought before him. Merlin at once saw the problem, which was not only in the fabric of the tower, but more so in its very foundation. For beneath the tower was a deep pool, and beneath the pool were two hollow stones, and within the stones lay two dragons.*

> *Now if this fable were to be applied to development today, especially rural development, then one of the two dragons would represent the relentless pursuit of a false economy which in turn is used to prove the standard of 'good' living. And the other dragon would be the increasing erosion of social life and well-being.*

The allusion to a story is a very clever trick to get readers 'hooked'. Few of us can resist the urge to know what happens next. The link to the subject of rural development is then made very neatly.

▶ Paragraphing and sentences

When checking on the style suitable for a particular magazine, one of the first things to do is to look at the length of paragraphs and sentences. The more serious or academic the magazine, the more its readers want to have ideas analysed in depth. That is likely to result in longer paragraphs. If, on the other hand, you are writing for a very popular magazine – or one for children – your paragraphs will need to be kept quite short.

It's worth actually counting the words of half a dozen sentences of an article in your chosen magazine to find the average sentence length. You may be surprised at the shortness of these in the simpler magazines. Here, there will be a definite upper word-limit which is seldom, if ever, crossed.

▶ Structure and links

Linking your paragraphs and topics will be even more important than in essays. Remember that anyone who has difficulty following an article in a magazine generally gives up and looks for something more interesting. So if you feel shaky on this one, check the sections on paragraphs and linking in chapter 6.

Unless you are writing for an academic journal, however, you will not usually need to construct as tight an argument as you would when writing an essay. Your structure in an article just needs to make your material clear and easy to follow. So you can group your facts in whatever order seems helpful.

▶ Language and style

The type of words you use and the way you construct your sentences are both crucial for ensuring that your article is suitable for the magazine you've chosen. This is much easier than it sounds. You may already have a good 'feel' for the magazine and be able to imitate the way its contributors write. It's a good idea to do a swift bit of analysis. Here's a checklist that may come in handy:

Analysing the language used in a particular magazine

- verbs — How lively are they?
- nouns — Do many of them fall into any particular category?
- register * — Is it formal, journalistic, technical, etc.?
- tone * — Is it serious, persuasive, friendly, helpful, conversational, etc.?

You might use this checklist to assess the opening of the article on Mrs Gruer. Words that strike me there are *residence, attendance, congenial, sustenance* and *purchasing*. Taken together, the three nouns and the adjective *congenial* give a traditional feel to the paragraph and set the scene for a gentle nostalgic trip into Scotland's past. Later in the article, once the writer has established his ground, the language becomes more relaxed.

In total contrast to this traditional piece, here's a paragraph from an article on second-hand bargains in German cars:

Keep it to yourself, but trade whispers reckon the 190 is a better car than its C-Class replacement, especially in terms of build quality and longevity. Despite its age, the 190 is still a winner. Like the Audi and BMW, it is disappointingly cramped in the rear. Mercedes equipment, also, is downright stingy. But you'll never wear the thing out.

Now check out this analysis:

- most sentences are short
- colloquialisms: *Keep it to yourself*
                    trade whispers
                    still a winner
- brief comments on specific items
- straight description, using *is*
- conversational tone – all the colloquialisms above/*downright stingy, you'll never wear the thing out.*

---

* For more information, see chapter 9.

This is sharp writing that gets its points across quickly in a very easy manner. We feel we are being given the lowdown by someone in the know. That easy manner, however, does not give way to loose writing. The piece is very carefully constructed.

Now look at Mark's third paragraph in his article, 'Sustainable Rural Development':

> *Looking at rural development one can only sigh with relief that most of the proposed £23 billion to be spent on road building was curtailed not by a government yielding under the enormous pressure of public opinion but by the fact that they actually did not have the money to proceed. The pressure came from people concerned about the threat to 160 Sites of Special Scientific Interest (SSSIs), 800 ancient monuments and countless beauty spots. But in the end, economics ruled the day. The irony is that the cost of destroying those sites would also have been added to the economic indicator, otherwise known as the Gross National Product.*

Once Mark has hooked his readers with the idea of a story, he moves straight into facts and figures. His style is clear but formal and he mixes concrete and abstract nouns (see chapter 4). He's writing for readers who are keen to learn about 'alternative' theories of living but who are also well-read and used to handling fairly complex material.

► Human interest

Almost all magazines apart from academic journals use the technique of relating subject matter to individual people in some form. This is a way of making a topic come alive and often of relating it directly to the reader.

The article that opens by telling us that Gladstone enjoyed getting away from Queen Victoria by going for long walks immediately causes us to sympathize with him. When we then find that he enjoys stopping off at Mrs Gruer's for some scones, we feel we almost know him. The article focuses on Mrs Gruer herself, and, before we realize it, we're feeling friendly towards her.

Although the article is ostensibly about Mrs Gruer, it is based on information about the Scottish Clearances in which many crofters were driven from their homes to make way for the country sports of landowners. The writer, Ian Mitchell, shows how the area of Inverey declined. He could have written an article full of facts, figures, and analysis. But he was not writing for an academic journal. So he concentrates on one individual in order to make the historical situation come alive.

We've already seen how Mark's article, 'Sustainable Rural Development', opens with a figure from myth. Now although myths tell us about heroes and tyrants, they are all rooted firmly in common human experience. Here, Merlin is seen to have a problem, and this links perfectly to what the writer wants to talk about: problems of rural planning. When we are shown Merlin with a problem, we subconsciously empathize with him because of all the problems we ourselves have encountered. Mark has very neatly prepared us to look at his article sympathetically.

In the second paragraph of his article on Plymouth, Bob Mann states:

> Whichever view you agree with, you must admit that everything is clean and well-kept ...

The writer has now begun to relate directly to the reader. He's using a conversational approach and so involving us closely in what he says. He treats us with respect, too, noting that we will have our own views on the subject. He is coming across as a charming guide to the city, and it's hard to resist accompanying him.

Putting yourself into your writing can be a real 'hook'. Most of us are nosy at heart, and we want to find out what others do and think. Of course, if you write about your own experiences they do need to be interesting or unusual – or you will need to have some idiosyncratic views on ordinary experiences.

If I were writing my article on language acquisition for the magazine, *Woman*, I could mention some of my experiences with my own children. This would make me sound friendly and approachable because I'd be revealing something about myself. From this, readers would be able to find themselves focusing with ease on a topic they might have found off-putting in a more academic format. I would have to be careful not to overdo it, however. Nobody wants to know all my pet theories on bringing up kids.

Perhaps the favourite person used in magazine articles nowadays is 'my friend'. When a writer wants to explain the value of couple counselling, we hear about 'my friends John and Sarah'. If the article is on finance, it'll be about 'my friend Tony, who didn't take advice before investing all his spare cash in one company'. If we're reading a piece on careers, we find ourselves fascinated by the life of 'my friend Sandra' which was transformed when she retrained as a vet.

Most of these people are, of course, fictional. Their function for the writer is to help get a message across, and it works extremely well. Readers focus on the human interest and are painlessly drawn into a consideration of the central subject matter. Check your chosen magazine to see whether this approach is used. But if 'my friend' isn't wanted, your own *true* experiences are almost always usable.

Another way of keeping your readers awake is to use snippets of conversation. These may be fictional too – or, if you have overheard some useful remarks, you can use those. They might need a little doctoring. Keep conversation brief and make sure it relates to important points.

▶ Title

Your title can be a good 'hook', and can demonstrate your ability to use language succinctly. The title for Ian Mitchell's article on Mrs Gruer relates directly to his reference to Queen Victoria. He called his piece, 'The Other Queen of Royal Deeside'. You need something brief, clear, punchy and new. It is quite easy to get the hang of this by leafing through your chosen magazine. Here are some examples from *Auto Express*:

> *Spirit of Adventure*
> *The Focus You've Been Waiting For*
> *Jensen Legend Returns*
> *Scores on Doors*

▶ Endings

Like openings, these can be tricky. An ending should tie things up neatly, leaving no loose ends. You might consider the following question:

> How do you want to leave your readers:
> > fired with enthusiasm?
> > calm?
> > understanding a new angle

on your topic?
aware of new facts?

It's a good idea to relate your closing remarks to the central ideas of your article – or perhaps to the beginning. Look at how Mark managed it in his article on rural development by referring to types of people he has discussed and linking all this back to his opening:

> These ... innovators of the future would ... be those people with special skills ... Because of their new relationship with nature and indeed their sense of belonging within nature they will bring about their own deep feelings of worthiness and trust in the future. Then the dragons of the past can be put to rest forever.

Problem solved!

SUMMARY

This chapter has covered:

- types of magazine
- choosing a magazine to write for
- planning
- researching your topic
- interviewing
- angling your topic to a magazine
- openings
- paragraphing and sentences
- links
- language and style
- human interest
- titles
- endings

13 Reports

INTRODUCTION

Report-writing involves the gathering of information, often for the purpose of discussion. This discussion is usually intended to lead to a change in the way something is done. Reports concentrate on the *gathering of facts*. This is so that those who read and discuss them can have a very clear picture of what is going on in a particular field.

You are likely to have to write reports if you are studying a science subject, business technology or social studies. The requirements for particular areas may be quite different, and it will be very important that you check out with your tutor exactly what is required for the particular task you've been given. In the world of work, things are different again. Some employers are happy with a restricted format. Once you are clued-up on the general nature of a report, however, it will be relatively easy to adjust to whatever is wanted. You may have been asked to write up a report from work you have already undertaken. In that case, you've already done a lot of the donkey-work.

The first section here – section I – shows you how to prepare to write a report. Section II is a guide to the items needed in a full-blooded report; and section III looks at the type of language required (which can be rather different from that used for essays). At the end of section II, you'll find a copy of a student report that was undertaken as an assignment on an Access to Higher Education course.

When you've got the hang of it, writing reports is not difficult, but you may find it a little confusing at first. So it would be a good idea to read right through this chapter before beginning any work for your report. This will ensure that you have an overall grasp of the method before you start to work out what goes where. The examples here are straightforward. With a little practice, you will be able to produce more sophisticated work.

I PREPARATION

The instructions you are given for writing a report may be quite lengthy. You are also likely to be given extra instructions and explanations verbally. If you happen to miss an introductory session, it's worth tracking your tutor down to check things out. When everyone is new to report-writing, it can be risky to rely on instructions relayed from another student. You don't want to incorporate someone else's confusion into your work.

▶ Your action plan

If you have been asked to write a report on an experiment that you've already conducted, you will already have most of the data you need, so turn straight to Section II. Generally, however, writing a report is likely to entail a good deal more legwork than writing an essay. Here you will be fact-finding rather than discussing issues. You may have less to worry about in terms of understanding complex concepts, but you are likely to need to cover more ground. You will also need to write more than one plan.

It's a good idea to begin any piece of work with a mind map to get your ideas flowing. (See the piece on mind maps in section I of chapter 6.) Your first plan, however, is likely to be an action plan rather a plan for your writing. Your action plan will show the various things that you need to do – and possibly the order in which you'll do them.

Let's suppose that you've been asked to write a report on the efficacy of the Bridge Centre – a new local centre for adults with learning difficulties. Your mind map might look something like this:

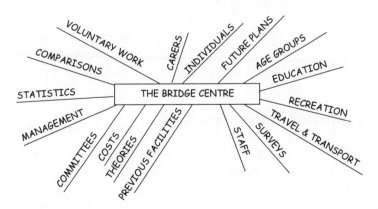

From this beginning, you might decide to plan your work as follows:

Interviews
>   *manager*
>   *users*
>   *officer from the local authority*
>   *health worker*
>   *education worker*
>   *carers/family members*
>   *voluntary workers*

Questionnaires
>   *staff – views/practice*
>   *adult users – likes/dislikes*

Data
>   *figures on   – number of users*
>   *– costings*

Reading
>   *sections of academic texts on learning disability*
>   *articles*
>   *reports on similar undertakings elsewhere*

Materials to be acquired
>   *site plan*
>   *copies of committee minutes*
>   *photographs of building*
>   *initial surveys of need in the area*
>   *copies of newspaper reports*

Having made your list, you may decide to put dates by which certain jobs need to be completed. You might spend a bit of time planning phone calls and visits. In chapter 12, you'll find a section on interviewing.

▶ Organizing your materials

Keeping your notes and other materials well organized will be really valuable for the writing stage. Any of the following can be useful for recording your findings:

- A4 paper
- cards (sorted alphabetically by topic)
- computer disks
- audiotapes.

Devise a method of sorting at the outset, and you'll save yourself hours later. A4 sheets can be kept in separate sections in ring binders, folders or old A4 envelopes; cards need a box; and disks and tapes need to be clearly labelled. A note on each item of what else it relates to – **cross-referencing** – will keep you on top of things.

While you are collecting your materials, it's best to ignore all the different headings of a report. The mind can't cope with two new processes at the same time. You'll be ready to think about the structure of the report when you've completed the fact-finding. Before doing any writing, re-check very carefully the title and instructions you've been given.

II THE STRUCTURE OF A REPORT

What follows is an explanation of each section of a traditional report. You may find that you are given an assignment which requires only *a few* of these sections; or you may find that you are given some headings that are slightly different from what you will see below. You may even be asked for some extras.

In essence, any report will contain the following items:

- a brief note on what's in it (the *Abstract*)
- an explanation of why and how it was set up (*Terms of Reference and Procedure*)
- a description of the things you found out (*Findings*)
- an analysis of what you found out (*Conclusions*)
- your suggestions for how things might be improved in the future (*Recommendations*).

One of the keys to good report-writing is clear separation of description, analysis and suggestions.

The sections of a full-blooded report are as follows:

Title-page

Abstract (sometimes called the 'Summary')
Contents
Terms of reference
Procedure (sometimes called 'Method')
Findings
Conclusions
Recommendations
Glossary
References
Bibliography
Appendices
Illustrations
Index

Don't worry. Everyone who is new to this finds it pretty mind-boggling. The system is very logical, however; and once you've completed your first effort, you'll have little difficulty with reports in the future.

▶ Title-page

This is a separate page containing just three things:

- the title or subject of the report
- the author's name
- the date the written report was completed.

▶ Abstract

This is a *very brief* summary of what is contained in the report. It will usually be no longer than one paragraph. An **abstract** is crucial for giving information. It enables anyone to find out, without having to plough through the whole thing, whether it is applicable to his or her field of work and therefore worth reading.

For example, imagine that you are a solicitor dealing with a client who is claiming that she was unfairly made redundant from her job with a large company. You want to find out something about that company's staffing policy, and you have managed to get hold of two reports. The titles of both are 'Staffing'. They are written by different authors on different dates. You turn to the page in the first that is labelled 'Abstract'. Here you find that this report describes a survey that catalogued numbers of employees by job title and geographical location. You look at the abstract for the second report and find that this one deals with revised staffing policy and redundancies. Clearly, this is the one you want to read.

An **abstract** is always written *after* the main body of the report has been completed. You won't be sure exactly what should go in your **abstract** until you've set out your **findings**, **conclusions** and **recommendations**.

▶ Contents

You will include this section only for reports that have a great many subsections. It is just a list of headings with appropriate page numbers. Its purpose is to make it easy for a reader to refer to separate items. The section on **findings**, for example, may have a number of subsections, each on a different topic. The **contents** enable anyone to turn directly to what he or she needs to read. This section should also contain a list of any illustrations, photographs, tables and graphs, with relevant page numbers.

▶ Terms of reference

In just a few lines, you will explain here the reason why the report was undertaken, who asked for it, and any guidelines that were given for conducting it. This can all seem like stating the obvious, but remember that the person who reads a report may know absolutely nothing of how it came to be written.

It can be very useful to know whether a report was written by an unbiased outsider or someone connected directly with the items covered. Knowing the reason why a report was written can also give readers valuable insight on the situation; and knowing the guidelines for gathering data will help people to assess whether the report is likely to contain the material they are interested in.

It's sometimes helpful to pretend, when writing all these sections, that you work for the police, and so to remember that every tiny piece of information must be recorded.

▶ Procedure

Here you explain how you went about gathering the information –
who you interviewed and why, what types of question you asked, what
you decided to include or exclude, and the places from which
information was gathered. Somebody glancing at your report might
decide whether to read further solely on the basis of what you
say here.

▶ Findings

This is likely to be your longest section. It will contain everything you
have found out – everything, that is, specifically related to the task
you've been given. Your **findings** will be what you have seen, heard
and read (and sometimes even what you have smelt and touched). As
with an essay, you must leave out anything that doesn't really fit the
criteria that were set for the assignment.

Unlike essays, however, reports benefit from being split up into
sections. You do not need to worry about links here as you would in an
essay; your task is just to make things crystal clear. So headings and
subheadings will be valuable tools in making your work clear and
easily readable.

This section must contain *nothing* of your own ideas or opinions.
Here you must act like a robot and record things exactly as you have
found them.

Your **findings** are likely to contain *some* of the following:

- information from any source you've consulted
- numerical data or results from questionnaires, experiments,
  published statistics, etc.
- details from letters and/or interviews, together with quotes.

Your task here is to describe very clearly what you have found out
without commenting on it.

Numbering can be an important aid to organizing your information.
If I were writing up my report on the Bridge Centre, my **findings** might
fall into four main categories:

1 *views of users*
2 *views of staff*

3 *activities provided*
4 *other centres.*

Each of these sections would be likely to have subsections, and these subsections might themselves have further subdivisions. Good headings and a clear system of numbering will keep sections clearly organised and easy to read. The structure of my **findings** might be something like this:

1 *Views of users*
    1.1 results of questionnaire
    1.2 information from interviews
    1.3 information from carers

2 *Views of staff*
    2.1 salaried staff on site
        2.1.1 manager
        2.1.2 other site staff
    2.2 visiting health workers

3 *Activities provided*
    3.1 details of educational classes
    3.2 figures on attendance

4 *Other centres*
    4.1 The Oak Tree Community Group
    4.2 The Sharp Centre
        4.2.1 mission statement
        4.2.2 summary of first annual report

In order to set out your **findings** clearly, you will need to construct a separate plan. Focus on your readers and concentrate on setting things out in the most user-friendly order that you can.

▶ Conclusions

This section will, in some ways, be like the end of an essay. Here you look at the facts you've found and weigh up what they mean and what consequences follow from them.

In essence, your conclusions will say something like:

The findings demonstrate that:

> *a* is the case
> *b* is the case
> *c* is the case.

You must be totally ruthless with yourself here and continue to keep to yourself your own opinion on what changes should be made.

If it seems helpful, you can reuse the headings you've used in your **findings**. My **conclusions** on the Bridge Centre report – given here briefly – might look something like this:

1 *Views of users*
The Centre is, in most respects, coming up to expectations. Responses on questionnaires to users showed a 95% satisfaction rate and responses from carers and families seems to back up this evidence of quality provision. Information from interviews was also extremely positive.

2 *Views of staff*
These are also positive in the main. The views of visiting health workers are broadly similar to those of the manager. Views of other site staff give valuable insight into issues such as the provision of lunches and other refreshments. Issues here could lead to dissatisfaction if not addressed.

3 *Activities provided*
Weekly timetables demonstrate a wide variety of facilities for users. The lack of take-up on some opportunities might seem to be a result of over-provision. Figures on attendance at education classes, however, suggest that this area of provision could usefully be expanded. The lower score on questions relating to sports activities suggests that this area is one which needs some improvement and perhaps an adjustment of policy.

4 *Other centres*
The Bridge Centre has had the benefit of both Lottery funding and the consequent design by prize-winning architects. Its facilities are of a far higher standard than those of the Oak Tree Community Group. The Sharp Centre, however, also has first-class premises and has been able to develop a particularly good system of client care.

▶ Recommendations

Ah, at last. It is here – and only here – that you can finally say some-thing of what you think should be done about the situation. This is where you make suggestions on how you think things should be changed for the future. You will be focusing on making *improvements*. There is still one constraint, however. Your views *must* be based clearly on your findings themselves.

Here are my **recommendations** for the Bridge Centre:

- *Discuss improved provision of lunches with caterers.*
- *Set up a user-group to provide feedback on curriculum and activities.*
- *Reconsider policy on sports activities, negotiate links with local fitness centre to provide volunteer coaching, and research possibility of visits from local sports personalities.*
- *Put on an extra maths class and a cookery workshop.*
- *Arrange for the manager from the Sharp Centre to give a presentation on client care to all staff at the Bridge Centre.*

Each of the points above begins with a verb (an action word – see Chapter 1). They all state that something particular should be *done*.

▶ Glossary

You may have had to include some technical terms in your report. A **glossary** lists these, giving definitions. It will be especially useful if the report is likely to be read by people who are not experts in your particular field. They are sure to need explanations.

▶ References

This is just another term for 'Notes'. These can appear either at the bottom of the relevant pages or in this section near the end (see chapter 7).

▶ Bibliography

This is a list of books, journals, other reports and so on that you have consulted while preparing your report. The purpose of a bibliography is to give readers some indication of the kind of ideas *behind* your work as well as to direct them to further reading on the subject (see chapter 7 – as above).

▶ Appendices

You will place here any material which you feel is valuable for anyone reading the report but which is not absolutely essential. This is likely to include tables, graphs, illustrations, and items such as correspondence that are too long and/or detailed to be included in the **findings**. You might like to think of an **appendix** as an overspill area. You may need more than one appendix in order to accommodate different issues.

▶ Illustrations

If you have used any illustrations, the sources for them will be listed here. The format of this section will be similar to the **references** section.

▶ Index

Include an **index** only in a very detailed report. As in any book, it's an alphabetical list, with page numbers, of all topics, names and technical terms that have appeared in the piece of work.

III EXAMPLE: A STUDENT'S REPORT

The following simple report was written by Kathleen for the Core Studies section of her Access to Higher Education course. Along with other students, she had completed a unit called 'Practical Writing'. For this unit, each student chose a topic related to his or her main subject and then submitted the following five pieces of work on it:

- a magazine article
- a letter to a broadsheet newspaper
- a leaflet
- a brochure
- a report.

The instructions for the report were as follows:

> Construct a questionnaire which will give you information on students' views of this unit and their experiences in writing the different sections. Conduct a survey using your questionnaire, and write up the responses in the form of a report.

REPORT ON CORE ENGLISH

PRACTICAL WRITING UNIT

Student Experiences

Kathleen Hardy

April 1998

Abstract

This is a report into the Practical Writing unit. It shows the students' views and opinions of the work they have been required to undertake. It also includes views and recommendations about the overall process.

Terms of reference

This report had to be made as a part of the Practical Writing unit for Core English. It has to show how this unit of study actually worked. The unit comprised five pieces of work: a letter to a broadsheet, a magazine article, a brochure, a leaflet and finally the report. All of these pieces of work had to be related to a main theme, which in turn had to be related to each student's main topic of study, either English Literature, Sociology, or Environmental Science.

Procedure

After completing many of the pieces of work in the Practical Writing unit, a list of questions was drawn up to gather information from the students about the work they had done. These questions were set out as a questionnaire. Each student then asked the questions to a number of other students individually, and by doing this, gathered data for this report.

Findings

a) Information/Research
It was found that a lot of research, for most students, had to be done. Of the twelve students questioned, ten felt that a lot of research was needed and two felt that they already had all the information needed.

b) Availability of Information
A number of places were used to gather information. Eight students used library services, three students had to contact organizations, which they found difficult and laborious doing, and one person needed to carry out a number of interviews for her data. Overall, most students found any information they'd needed easy to get hold of.

c) Classwork
It was found that all students were glad that some work, especially the letter and the brochure, was able to be done in class time.

d) Topic Choice

The students were asked if they found it easy or difficult to choose a topic for this unit. Out of those questioned, seven said that they'd found it easy, and five found the choosing of the topic very difficult. Out of those five, three had to choose a topic relating to English Literature, and the other two had to choose a topic relating to Environmental Science.

e) Style of Writing

The data collected showed that nine students found changing their style of writing for each piece of work difficult. However, three students had found it relatively easy. Also, all twelve students noted that they had learnt a lot about changing their style of writing for different purposes in this unit.

Conclusions

a/b) Information

It can be seen from the findings that the information collected, and research which needed to be done was quite easy for all students. Although difficulty was found by some in contacting various organizations.

c) Classwork

The most useful and helpful aid while undertaking this unit appeared to be the class time allocated to actually producing parts of the work.

d) Topic Choice

It would appear that the choosing of the main topic area was easiest for the Sociology students, and secondly for the Environmental Science students. The English Literature students had most difficulty in choosing a topic for this unit.

e) Style of Writing

From the findings it can be seen that the Practical Writing unit taught the students a lot about differing styles of writing and how it had to change and adapt to suit each piece of work. This was found hard to do.

Recommendations

a/b) Information
It would be beneficial to have a list of addresses of various national and local, well-known organisations available to students.

c) Classwork
If more class time could be made available to actually produce items of work for this unit, then this would be very useful.

d) Topic Choice
Extra advice and help would benefit those who have to choose a topic relating to English Literature and maybe Environmental Science.

e) Style of Writing
Although the importance of learning how to change styles of writing was appreciated by the students, understanding the practicalities of actually changing their own style was felt to be rather vague, and therefore students would need more help in achieving this to a greater degree.

Feedback on Kathleen's report

Terms of reference
The first two sentences are fine. The next two describe the unit, so they would be better used as an introduction to **findings**.

Findings
These are very clearly set out and consequently easy for a reader to follow.

Conclusions
Kathleen has followed the headings she used for her **findings**, so this section, too, is very easy to follow. Here she explains what the results of her survey show up.

Recommendations
Again following her main headings, Kathleen has made very clear suggestions for the future.

IV THE LANGUAGE OF REPORTS

Decisions we make on the language we use in a report are just as important as those we make when writing letters or articles. Reports need to be really clear and straightforward. So focus on making things easy for whoever is going to be reading your report. You might like to look back at how I described putting oil in my car in the section 'Describing a process' (chapter 9). I concentrated there on making things easy for someone who was new to the process. I showed every single step of the job, used simple language as much as possible, and kept my sentences fairly short. That style of writing is ideal for reports (except for the use of the word *I*) (see 'Active v. Passive', below).

You will have found that in writing essays, you need to put your emotions in cold storage. When writing reports, you need to bury your feelings six feet down in solid ice. I suggested under **findings** that you write like a robot. I wasn't joking. Your language should be:

- clear and concise
- objective
- unemotional
- jargon-free (wherever possible)
- impersonal.

Obviously, you will do a *rough draft*. This is the point at which you must prune out all unnecessary statements and any flowery descriptions. Until you reach your **recommendations**, you need to be totally unbiased. This means that from the very beginning – when you are planning how to conduct your report – you must put personal feelings to one side.

▶ Active v. passive (see chapter 1)

Your tutors may accept essays that include comments in the first person – that is, using the word *I*; reports, however, have traditionally been written impersonally. The reasons for this are to prevent emotion creeping in and to concentrate on the facts. This means that a statement such as

I interviewed employees in three different occupations.

is better if changed to:

Employees in three different occupations were interviewed.

A statement in your **recommendations**, such as

I feel that further training is essential for operators of machines

is better as:

Operators of machines should be given further training.

In these examples I have changed the verbs from active to passive. Educational practice is itself undergoing a great deal of change at present, however, and you may find that your tutor would prefer you to concentrate on getting your facts and structure right rather than worrying too much about passive verbs.

▶ Reported speech

If you have carried out interviews, you are likely to want to report what one or two people said. Use chapter 5 to help you here.

▶ Tense

Reports are written largely in the past tense (see chapter 1). Obviously, since you are describing what you found out, you are bound to use the past tense a great deal. When you are talking about processes that are continuing, however, you are going to need to use the present tense.

▶ Clarity

It's important that anyone reading your report should find it clear and easy to follow. So use technical terms only when necessary, keeping your language as straightforward as possible. You might like to look at the section on describing a process in chapter 9. This will remind you to make your writing even more straightforward than seems necessary. If you have a complex process to describe, it can sometimes help to draw a rough diagram of this and then to use it to remind yourself of all the stages that need to be mentioned. Keep your sentences short. It's no bad thing to make your report sound really simple.

SUMMARY

This chapter has covered:

- your action plan
- organizing your material
- the sections of a full-blown report:
    Title-page
    Abstract (sometimes called the 'Summary')
    Contents
    Terms of reference
    Procedure (sometimes called 'Method')
    Findings
    Conclusions
    Recommendations
    Glossary
    References
    Bibliography
    Illustrations
    Index
- the key sections of a report:
    a brief note on what's in it (the *abstract*)
    an explanation of why and how it was set up (*terms of refer-ence and procedure*)
    a description of the things you found out (*findings*)
    an analysis of what you found out (*conclusions*)
    your suggestions for how things might be improved in the future (*recommendations*)
- the language of reports:
    clear and concise
    objective
    unemotional
    jargon-free (wherever possible)
    impersonal
    reported speech

14 Exam Essays

INTRODUCTION

The best time to read this chapter is when you are within two or three months of your exams. It is unlikely to be of much use to you a year before you sit them. You will only depress yourself if you start worrying about exams too early. The main reason for this is that, while there is still a lot of new material to cover, you really are in no position either to have an overall grasp of a year's work or to focus your mind on what is, in fact, a totally different undertaking from writing coursework essays.

This is not to be confused with finding out what the course itself will cover. You really do need to know that. It's also a good idea to find out what general areas you will be tested on in the exam. You can then make sure that you cover these thoroughly during the year.

By the way, some people get worried about what seems to be the highly formal language in which exam questions are often written. There's actually nothing to fear here. The questions are very carefully constructed so that, hopefully, they cannot be misunderstood. This can make them sound very formal – rather like legal jargon. It can tend to make the questions *appear* more difficult than they actually are. As with term-time essays, the questions that look difficult are often easier to answer than those that seem simple. This is because a question that gives you a very tight structure to work to can actually help you to bring out all the things you know in a highly organized manner.

Writing an exam essay is a totally different task from writing assignments – which are designed to enable you to *learn*. Term-time essays cannot be written without doing research, reading relevant material, and spending a good deal of time thinking. These assignments test your coverage of an area of work and your ability to construct a meaningful discussion of it. *The fact that you probably have two or three weeks in which to think about this is taken into account by whoever marks your work.* Exams are quite different.

The purpose of an exam is to give you the opportunity to show *some* of the things you've learnt during the year and to enable you to demonstrate that you can select relevant points from what you know in order to answer specific questions *in a short space of time.* Nobody can possibly remember everything that has been covered on a course, and nobody can write all there is to know on a topic in under an hour.

This chapter will first look briefly at how to revise for exams. It will then explain how to go about tackling an exam essay. This will be followed by an example of a student's answer in a mock exam.

▶ The revision process

Taking bite-sized chunks is the name of the game here. You will need to go through all your lecture notes, class notes, handouts and any photocopied material you possess. Take these items one at a time. Your task is to read each through once, pencil or highlighter in hand. Each time you come to a key point, either circle or highlight it. Sometimes a tutor will have written one or two useful points on your essay; so highlight these too.

After *one* reading and highlighting, **list** the points you've found on a fresh sheet in as few words as possible. Do this with everything, and read nothing twice. Fit in a short session of this work whenever you have a spare 15 minutes and work as fast as you can.

All you have to do after that (as they say on children's TV) is to condense all your lists into as few sheets of paper as possible and to colour-code the topic areas. Stick to key points and key words. Aim to note ideas and trends where possible rather than overloading yourself with too many facts. Draw mind maps or diagrams whenever you can because these are easier to remember than lists. If you are able to add drawings, these will be even better memory aids.

When you have done all this, you will have revisited all the main areas of your course. You will be getting well prepared for your exams. Keep going over your master lists, and practise trying to write them out from memory. If you have any spare time now, have a go at writing answers to past papers – or make up questions of your own.

▶ Planning and writing the exam essay

Analysing the question
The best way to start is:

1 underline or highlight the *key words* in the question
2 write a quick *list or mind map*
3 *plan the order* in which you'll deal with your points.

This is a potted version of your procedure for term-time essays. Never, *ever*, leave out the first stage here. In an exam, most of us are under stress. If ever we are going to misread something, it will be during an exam. Underlining key words forces us to focus on what is necessary.

The procedure for coping with an exam essay is common to all subjects. I'm going to suppose that I'm a student on an introductory course in contemporary studies and that I have to answer the following question:

Explain and discuss what seem to you to be the main issues for environmental policies in the next 15 years.

When I've underlined the key words, the question will look like this:

<u>Explain</u> and <u>discuss</u> what <u>seem to you</u> to be the <u>main issues</u> for <u>environmental policies</u> in the <u>next 15 years</u>.

You'll notice that, as with ordinary essays, I've underlined a large percentage of the question. I've also underlined the words *explain* and *discuss*. Those two words are the **instructions**. They are vital because they tell you *how* to deal with the question. If I omitted to underline them, I'd be likely to forget to give an explanation and I might omit to show more than one side of each issue.

By underlining, I've made myself fully aware that I absolutely *must* take the following four issues into consideration:

1 my own views
2 main issues
3 environmental policies
4 the next 15 years.

Organizing your ideas

I'd start with a rough list of the topics I could cover:

> *global warming*
> *ozone depletion*
> *population increase*
> *destruction of biodiversity*
> *recycling*
> *atmospheric pollution*
> *GM crops*
> *rising sea levels*
> *industrial waste*

The fact that the question asks for my own views and the *main issues* means that I must show that I can rate some topics as more important than others. So I'll have to cut down my list:

> *global warming*
> ~~*ozone depletion*~~
> *population increase*
> *destruction of bio-diversity*
> ~~*recycling*~~
> ~~*atmospheric pollution*~~
> ~~*GM crops*~~
> ~~*rising sea levels*~~
> *industrial waste*

Selection is crucial. I am not likely to gain many marks if I just write down everything I know on a topic. I must choose just those items that relate specifically to the question. I will also need to show that I understand the issues involved. I will not be expected to put forward my personal pet theories. In fact, doing that could even lose me marks. I must concentrate on what I've been taught on the main issues.

I've managed now to find four main headings. This is a sensible number to cope with in an exam. You can see that I've also managed to include two other items from my list under these headings:

> 1 *global warming* –   *rising sea levels*
> 2 *destruction of biodiversity* –   *GM crops*
> 3 *population increase*
> 4 *industrial waste*

Now that I've got a rough plan, I can begin to write. I can tick the points off my list as I cover them.

Starting off
In an exam, there is no time for long introductions. I've been asked for *main issues*, so I can begin my answer by stating these:

> *The main environmental issues that will have to be tackled by governments and both national and transnational organizations involved in policy-making in the next 15 years are global warming, the destruction of biodiversity, population increase and industrial waste.*

That's clear and simple. Now I can take the items one at a time, explaining them and discussing their relative importance and their effects on landscape, economics, demography,* and so on.

The middle
This is where I must show specific and/or technical knowledge. I need to demonstrate that I *understand* the issues I refer to. Each separate issue will need at least one paragraph. It's a good idea to give yourself some practice in writing exam answers so that you can get a feel for how much data you can get down in the time available.

As I write, I must quickly look back *several times* at the question in order to check that I'm still on track. In this particular essay, I must remember to relate whatever I say to:

> environmental policies
> the next 15 years.

This is the sort of thing that is very easily forgotten. I could get stuck into my main topic areas and omit to mention policies or timescales. It would be sensible to think of both local *and* global policies and of both short *and* long-term measures.

The argument
Just as with a term-time essay, it's important to explain *how* what you say relates to the question you've been given. Show the relevant facts

---

* The study of the size and distribution of populations.

that you know, explain how they affect the particular situation you've been asked to write on, and give what seems to you to be the most sensible view of it all. It's fatally easy to assume that because you've written down the relevant facts, argument is implicit. It isn't. You *must* spell out the implications and what you think about them. Different students often take very different angles on the same set of facts. Make sure you explain the situation as *you* see it.

Linking
Just as in essays written throughout the year, linking is important both for your argument and to help the reader follow your explanations. A simple link sentence at the beginning of each paragraph will demonstrate your intentions.

For example, if I'd begun a section on GM crops by giving points *against* them, I'd need to go on to give points in their favour, in order to demonstrate that I had a clear grasp of the issue. I might begin my next paragraph like this:

> *There are, however, studies that show that GM crops are no threat to the environment. Perhaps their greatest positive benefit will be provision of food for the Third World ...*

If I had begun with the *positive* points, I might begin my ensuing paragraph like this:

> *There is, however, a high level of public concern over GM crops, especially in Britain. Growers of organic crops have found that pollen from test sites can be carried to plants several miles away ...*

Each point I make must be spelt out really clearly so that whoever marks my essay will know exactly what I mean. I would need, of course, to add specific examples in order to illustrate what I say.

Conclusions
As with introductions, there's not much time for these in exams. But it's important to sum up what you've said on the various issues and to underline where you stand. My conclusion to the essay on environmental policies might look like this:

> *The issue of industrial waste is pressing because of its widespread effects. It would also seem crucial to develop policies at once that*

will address issues of reduced biodiversity, since this is not merely a cosmetic issue but will ultimately affect the structure of the natural world on which we depend. Population increase is an issue that is both sensitive and crucial. The developed world has not yet suffered unduly from overpopulation; but population issues in other nations are increasingly likely to have global effects. Without specific policies, Third World nations will always be the ones who suffer most from scarce resources. The next five to ten years will be crucial for long-term planning. Perhaps the toughest problem we face, however, is global warming. Governments must collaborate on policy here for the long term. Without co-operation on this, the efficacy of all other policies will be in jeopardy.

Budgeting your time

If your exam lasts three hours and consists of three essay questions, expect to write approximately three to four sides of A4 for each answer. Your tutors will almost certainly have explained that you need to budget your time *very* carefully in an exam. It's only common sense to expect to spend longest on questions that carry the most marks. For questions carrying the same marks, however, the following is a well-known fact:

The combined marks for one really good answer and one poor answer are generally less than the combined marks for two average answers.

So don't make the mistake of spending extra time on your best topic. It really is essential to balance your time if you are to maximize your chances of success.

Language

Generally speaking, you will not need to worry about writing wonderful sentences. Getting your answers on paper is quite enough to think about. Indeed, time spent in careful crafting of your language in an exam is likely to be time wasted. The tutor who marks your script will be working fast. He or she will be looking for facts and for sensible comment on them. If you are studying English, however, your grammar will be important.

The best language is clear and simple. If you've been working on improving the way you write, this will certainly pay dividends in the exam. If you've not had a chance to do this, and your exams are due soon, aim to keep your sentences fairly short so that there's less chance of getting into difficulties. As with any piece of work, leaving a line between paragraphs will help to make your answers look clear and well organized.

▶ Example: a student's exam essay

You will find below a student essay from a mock examination. Mocks are *not* set in order to see how high you can score. Their purpose is to give you a practice run. You will get valuable feedback that will enable you to cope more easily when you come to the real thing. It's quite possible to do badly in a mock exam and then to pass the main exam.

The essay below was written by Pat, an evening-class student on an A-level English course. One of the books on her syllabus was *Great Expectations*. She had a choice of two questions in this section of her exam paper. This is the one she chose to answer:

> *Explain some of the things that Pip learnt in his journey to adulthood.*

For those who don't know the story, I must explain that it was written by Charles Dickens in the mid-nineteenth century. The orphaned Pip lives with his sister, known as Mrs Joe, and her husband, Joe Gargery, the local blacksmith. A chance meeting with a convict, Magwitch, to whom the child Pip gives some food, has unexpected consequences. The convict makes money in Australia and becomes Pip's anonymous benefactor. Pip is given fine clothes and sent off to London to live a life of culture and ease. He overspends wildly, and finally has to confront the provider of his cash. He learns, you won't be surprised to hear, many lessons.

It is possible to learn a great deal on how to write exam essays by looking at Pat's answer. She has filled it with facts and has also added plenty of comment to show that she understands the *implications* of the issues she refers to.

Pat's mock exam answer
One of the important things Pip learned on his journey to full maturity was that having money wasn't everything. He realized that although he had money, he couldn't automatically get all he wanted and the main thing he desired was Estella. He realized that he had

to work hard at being a gentleman and it did not come easily to him. He learned that he shouldn't forget his roots and his upbringing. He also learned about love and respect for those who had helped him in the past.

Pip also learned about morality and in the end realized how badly he had treated Joe and Biddy. Through Jaggers, the lawyer, he realized how unfair the justice system was to poor people because it was so corrupt. Jaggers had people twisted around his little finger and Pip learned how badly treated criminals were if they had no money because Compeyson always got away with much lighter sentences than Magwitch. Through helping Herbert he learned the true meaning of what a gentleman was, and how important kindness and decency were and by doing this he became a morally better person.

His relationship changed with many characters in the novel. Pumblechook used to use Pip as a whipping post and referred to him as "swine" when he was young. However, after he found Pip had a benefactor and was to become a gentleman Pumblechook's relationship with Pip changed altogether. He believed Pip's expectations were due to him because he had introduced Pip to Miss Havisham. He continually wanted to shake Pip's hand and kept saying "May I?"

Although Pip has little feeling for his sister, Mrs Joe, who treated him cruelly, he was very shocked when he returned to the forge and found she had been attacked.

Pip's relationship also changed with Joe. He loved him dearly in the beginning and always thought of him very fondly and wanted nothing more than to become his apprentice. However, after he went to London Pip became rather ashamed and embarrassed about Joe. When Joe came to visit, Pip behaved very snobbishly and felt very uncomfortable especially when Joe kept referring to him as "Sir". When Pip returned to where he'd lived as a child, he stayed at the Blue Boar Inn because he didn't want to stay with Joe and Biddy. He only returned to visit for the funeral of Mrs Joe. In the end though, Pip realized how stupid he had been to try to forget his past and felt very guilty about neglecting Joe who had always been so kind.

When Pip first met Wemmick he was unsure of him because Wemmick would only shake hands with "the Aged" and those awaiting trial. Pip thought he was a very small and "dry" little man. This changed when Pip saw the other half of Wemmick's life at home and he became a good friend and provided a lot of information for Pip. Pip enjoyed his company on his visits to Walworth.

When Pip first met Biddy he liked her and imagined falling in love and marrying her, that was until he encountered Estella. Once he had met Estella he treated Biddy rather badly by pouring out to her how he felt about Estella. When he realized Estella wouldn't love him he again imagined settling down with Biddy, but she knew that he would never be happy with her, although she loved him very much. At the end Pip had resigned himself to returning to the forge and marrying Biddy after all but Joe beat him to it. Pip, however, still hoped they would be happy and realized how badly he had treated them.

Feedback

Pat's answer is full of good points about *Great Expectations*. She has demonstrated that she's read the book carefully and knows it well. She constantly refers to various characters and to specific episodes in the story. These are her **facts**. As she goes along, she gives her **analysis** of Pip's behaviour. **Facts** and **analysis** will be essential in any essay you write in an exam.

In my comments I suggested to Pat that her essay would have benefited from the following:

(a) an explanation of Pip's relationship with the convict Magwitch
(b) a discussion of Pip's relationship with Miss Havisham
(c) the inclusion of a plan.

(a) Pat may have felt that explaining Pip's relationship with the convict was unnecessary because it was obvious. Well, just as with term-time essays, you can only be given marks for what you actually put on paper. You do not need to go into great detail about everything you mention, but you do need to show that you are fully aware of the implications.

Central to *Great Expectations* is Pip's journey from childhood innocence through snobbishness to eventually being able to return the love shown him by society's outcast, Magwitch. It was important to indicate how the relationship with Magwitch came about. A couple of sentences would have been sufficient for this.

(b)   Miss Havisham, the lady of a local country house, is also a significant figure in Pip's journey. She allows Pip to believe that she was the anonymous donor of his wealth, and she encourages Estella – with whom he falls in love – to treat him with disdain. Pip learns a great deal about life and love as a result of Miss Havisham's actions. The fact that he attempts to save her from a fire, and gets burnt himself in the process, demonstrates his emerging sense of responsibility towards others. It was essential to include a discussion of Miss Havisham's role in Pip's journey to adulthood.

(c)   Pat may have made a rough plan on her question paper, but she has not shown it here. It is essential to include a plan on your answer paper. It has two functions:

- it keeps you organized and focused
- it demonstrates your knowledge.

If, by any chance, you don't have time to finish a question, there may be something on your plan which gets you another mark or two. It could even make the difference between passing and failing.

    Here are some points about specific items in Pat's essay:

- Notice how she gets straight into the meat of the question. She's therefore picking up marks from the word go.
- In her third paragraph, Pat refers to the character Pumblechook. What she says about him is quite right, but notice how she is mistakenly focusing on him here instead of on Pip. She needed to explain what *Pip* learns from this relationship because that is what the question has asked her.
- Pat's last sentence about Pip's relationship with Joe – in paragraph 5 – is good. It sums up all she's said in this paragraph, and makes clear that she understands what Pip has learnt.
- The explanation of Pip's relationship with Wemmick needed a little more comment. Pat needed to spell out exactly what Pip learnt.
- The essay needs a brief conclusion.

SUMMARY

This chapter has covered:

- revision
    - work in **bite-sized chunks**
    - **highlight key points** from your notes, essays, handouts, etc.
    - **make master lists/mind maps**
- planning your exam essay
    - highlight or underline **key words**
    - make a **list or mind map**
    - **plan the order** of your main points
    - **budget your time**
- writing your exam essay
    - write a *very brief* **introduction**
    - give *at least* one **paragraph for each issue**
    - include: **examples**
                explanation
                argument (i.e. show what seems to you the most sensible line to take)
    - tie things up in a brief **conclusion**

Appendix
Spelling Strategies

If you have *severe* problems with spelling, ask one of your tutors to recommend a book that will give you specific help or tell you where to find a drop-in class for English skills. You might also look at the section on **dyslexia** at the start of this book. If, however, you are like many people and know that your spelling just isn't very good, you'll find some tips here to help you. People learn in different ways, so use the methods that suit you best.

The main thing is to attack the problem consciously. For some years, I think I must have hoped that I would somehow imbibe the correct spellings of words from the atmosphere. Later, I realized I'd have to take positive steps, and I started to use a dictionary. It wasn't until I started to teach that I found that there are lots of useful tricks you can use to help you remember how to spell particular words. Memory aids (and they can be used for anything you want to remember) are called **mnemonics** (for pronunciation, ignore the '*m*'). See below.

▶ The computer spell-check

If you are able to use a computer, you may find its spell-check facility useful. This will pick up a lot of misspellings and improve the look of your assignments. But there are certain things to beware of. A computer won't recognize many technical words and will change some things you may have spelt correctly to the closest word it knows. It may also be set up for American spelling, which is fine if you live in America, but not much help if you're in Britain. It's usually possible, however, to change the language setting to the one you need.

The main problem with relying solely on a spell-check facility is that you won't be improving your own spelling. This won't matter during the year, but can leave you at a serious disadvantage when you come to exams. You'll probably get the best value from a spell-checker by using it *in conjunction with* your own programme of spelling improvement.

▶ Mnemonics

You may already know the mnemonic for remembering whether to put *i* before *e* in the middle of a word:

i before *e* except after *c*

This functions whenever the sound is *ee*. The mnemonic has a strong rhythm to it, and it's this that makes it easy to remember. So we can work out (without having to learn them) how to spell words like

retrieve
⎫
⎬ the *i* does not follow a *c*
⎭
achieve

and

conceit
⎫
⎬ the *e* must go next to the *c*
⎭
deceive

Exceptions are words like *eight* and *seize*.
The key to a good mnemonic is to make it:

- simple
- enjoyable
- amusing.

If you can add a mental picture, that's even better. If you want to remember how to spell the word *mnemonic*, try this:

m	n	e	+ monic
mind	**N**ed's	**e**lephant	

You might visualize a tiny man with a huge, ungainly elephant.
It doesn't matter what you choose as long as it will stick in your mind. The more bizarre your mnemonics, the easier they will be to remember. Allow yourself to fantasize. Yes, even sex can help here.

▶ Your personal spelling aid

Another very valuable tool for learning to spell well is a notebook. Divide each page into two down the middle. On the left, keep a running list of words you have misspelt:

- check the dictionary for the correct spelling
- underline the letter or section of the word that has been causing you problems.

In the right-hand column:

- note down a mnemonic for each one.

Have this notebook handy whenever you are writing an assignment.

You will need to take especial care over names and technical words related to your own subject. You might use the back of your notebook for these.

▶ Visualizing a word

Some people find that if they spend a few moments looking at a word and then close their eyes, they can see it clearly in their mind's eye. If this works for you, do use this method for learning. It's quick and simple.

▶ Spotting the parts of a word

Sometimes, you can clearly see that a word has several sections to it. So you can remember its spelling more easily by splitting it up. For example:

prom	is	es	promises
fluc	tu	ate	fluctuate
car	til	age	cartilage

You will find more on parts of words in the sections below on **prefixes** and **suffixes**.

▶ Saying words aloud

When you are alone, try saying difficult words aloud, using a sing-song voice and really exaggerating each section of the word. You can devise chants, too. For example, the word *necessary* is often misspelt. Try chanting "One *c* and two *s*'s in *ne – ces – sary*" to help you remember.

▶ Some typical problem areas

You will need to know the following terms for this section:

Vowel   a, e, i, o, u

Consonant   any letter *except* those above*

Prefix   an addition to the beginning of a word, e.g.
                 *re*turn/*un*do

Suffix   an addition to the end of a word – e.g.
                 loud*ly*/sense*less*

Syllable   one section of a word, containing a vowel, that
                 could function as one 'beat'. E.g. in *particularly*
                 there are five beats: *par   tic   u   lar   ly*
                 (I like to count beats on my fingers)

There are many rules for English spelling, but it's certainly not necessary to remember them all in order to spell well. Sometimes, however, people find them handy, so I'll give two here to start you off. The first one is really easy. You may already know it.

The plural of words ending in *y*
A word that ends with the letter *y* is made plural by changing the *y* to *ie* before adding *s*. For example:

Singular   *Plural*
city   cities

---

* The letter *y* can function as both a consonant and a vowel.

lady	ladies
body	bodies

Unfortunately, of course, there are one or two exceptions. But, in this case, they are not difficult to remember. Words that have a vowel *before* the *y* don't change. For example:

donkey	donkeys
monkey	monkeys
tray	trays
boy	boys

Double letters

Remembering whether or not to use a double letter can be a real bugbear. For a difficult word where the double letter is somewhere in the middle, the best thing is to copy it out, split it into syllables, and devise a suitable mnemonic.

Other problem areas for knowing whether or not to double a letter are prefixes and suffixes.

PREFIXES

These are easy. When adding a prefix to a word, just slot it straight on. Sometimes, this will mean that you end up with a double letter, sometimes it won't. For example:

moderate	**im**moderate
noticed	**un**noticed
marine	**sub**marine
terrestrial	**extra**terrestrial

SUFFIXES

Don't double the letter when adding a suffix beginning with a vowel to

- a two-syllable word where the stress is on the *first* syllable, e.g.:

*mar*ket	market**ed**

---

* the study of the size and distribution of populations

*bud*get   budget**ed**

Do double the letter when adding a suffix beginning with a vowel to

- a two-syllable word where the stress is on the *second* syllable, e.g.:

    ad*mit*   admitt**ed**
    de*ter*   deterr**ed**

- a one-syllable word that ends in a vowel followed by a consonant, e.g.:

    trim   trimm**ed**
    spot   spott**ed**

Note: words of two syllables ending in l: This can depend on where you live, e.g.:

    British spelling: travel   travell**ed**
    American spelling: travel   travel**ed**

Commonly misspelt words
Here's a list of some words that are very frequently misspelt. It isn't exhaustive, but should get you thinking. You might like to put them in your spelling notebook.

accommodate	gauge
achieve	independent(ly)
acknowledge	necessary
address	occur(red)
argument	persuade
business	possession
committee	prejudice
definite(ly)	privilege
embarrassed	recommend
existence	receipt
extremely	separate(ly)
February	until
fulfil*(led)	usually

---

* The American spelling of this word is *fulfill*.

Common confusions

accept	receive or agree to
except	apart from, with the exception of
affect	change in some way
effect	the result of something

If I spend less, this will have an *affect* on my bank balance. Hopefully, the final *effect* will be that I clear my debts.

practice (noun)	the usual way of doing something or the repetition of an activity (often for improvement)
practise (verb)*	to do (something) repeatedly to gain skill

John *practises* the guitar every evening.
It's John's *practice* to play the guitar every evening after he's had something to eat.

principal	head of a college, director, or most important person in a company
principle	standard by which people behave or a natural law governing the behaviour of a body or system

The college *principal* prides himself on his *principles*.

their (possession)	e.g. their essays
there (place)	e.g. over there
they're (contraction)	they are
to	Mel went *to* France.
two	Mel has *two* cousins.
too	Mel is *too* busy to clean the car.
where (place)	Tim remembered where he'd left the wrench.
were (verb)	Tim and Mick *were* having a drink.

---

*The American spelling for this is *practice*.

could've (contraction) – could have
would've (contraction) – would have

These last two are very frequently written incorrectly as *could of* and *would of.* The reason this happens is because of what we hear. It can sound as though the word *of* is at the end of *could've* and *would've.*

Answers

Chapter 1

Activity 1
1 wash
2 foretell
3 long
4 migrate
5 sends
6 desire

Activity 2
1 daydreams
2 works
3 delivers
4 like
5 pray
6 exports

Activity 3
1 past
2 present
3 past
4 future
5 present
6 past perfect
7 future
8 present
9 future
10 past perfect

Activity 4
1 present
2 past
3 future
4 future continuous
5 present continuous
6 past perfect
7 future continuous
8 past
9 past perfect continuous
10 past continuous

Activity 5
1 d
2 h
3 d
4 d
5 b
6 b
7 h
8 h
9 d
10 b

Activity 6

1	A	6	P
2	P	7	P
3	P	8	P
4	A	9	A
5	A	10	P

Chapter 2

Activity 1
2, 3, 7

Activity 2

	Subject	verb
1	Jimi Hendrix	died
2	Beatlemania	swept
3	Fraser	plays
4	Punk Rock	lasted
5	Many young girls	have wanted
6	Salsa	is becoming

Activity 3

1 Lucy ran home, crying all the way.
  Lucy ran home. She cried all the way.
2 Ken's dog had been annoying the neighbours, barking all morning.
  Ken's dog had been annoying the neighbours. It had been barking all morning.
3 Brad ran down the road with the cheque, laughing all the way to the bank.
  Brad ran down the road with the cheque. He laughed all the way to the bank.
4 The children came home covered in mud looking absolutely filthy.
  The children came home covered in mud. They looked absolutely filthy.
5 English grammar can be difficult, causing all sorts of problems.
  English grammar can be difficult. It can cause all sorts of problems.
6 I couldn't think how to get the cork out of the bottle. I had tried everything I knew.
  Or I couldn't think how to get the cork out of the bottle. I had been trying everything I knew.

7 The wolf set off through the forest looking for the cottage belonging to Little Red Riding Hood's grandmother.
The wolf set off through the forest. He was looking for the cottage belonging to Little Red Riding Hood's grandmother.

Activity 4

1 Nursery schools are places where children learn some of the basic skills they will need for primary school. These include recognizing their names, making simple models, and getting along with others.
2 My local school has started a monthly newsletter. Teachers believe that this will help make local people more aware of all the activities available for children and parents. (You might have kept the original wording and put a comma after *newsletter*.)
3 This essay will look at both sides of the argument in order to show the complexity of the issues involved. These are crucial issues, affecting every aspect of our lives.

Activity 5

1 Carl
2 Ron
3 the cowboy
4 Pam
5 a belt of rain, high winds
6 Maxine
7 The children, the buns
8 To work at a satisfying job

Activity 6

1 the casino
2 the suspects
3 their winnings
4 a fight
5 the events
6 calm

Activity 7

1 you
2 class IV
3 her client
4 us
5 me

Chapter 3

Activity 1

1 Marian has travelled in France, Spain, Australia, India and the USA. (It is OK to put a comma after *India* if you wish.)
2 We were watched by a lean, ageing kangaroo.
3 After two weeks on buses and trains, it was a relief to smell sea air.

4 Jason, our guide, walked fast and spoke little.
5 Air disasters, it is well known, are fewer than accidents on the roads.
6 Taking a foreign holiday, despite problems with accommodation, currency and language, can be a liberating experience. (It would not be wrong to put a comma after *currency*. Since there is little chance of a misunderstanding, however, it's probably best to omit it.)
7 Day after day, the grey rocks, dotted here and there with small plants, formed a backdrop for our trek.
8 Taking a foreign holiday can be a liberating experience. (It would be wrong to put any commas in number 8 because there is no extra information in the sentence. This is similar to the sentence *Maria went for a long walk across the fields to the river*. Everything here is part of the main statement. It's also the case that the phrase *Taking a foreign holiday* is the subject of the sentence, so it mustn't be separated from its verb.)

Activity 2
The full stops after 'freedom' and 'reactionary' could be replaced by semicolons. In the first case, you might decide to keep within one sentence the statements concerning the two views on the motor car. In the second case, you could keep together the explanations of the difficulties in which governments can find themselves.

Activity 3
1 It's only when I laugh that it hurts. (contraction)
2 It's a lovely day today. (contraction)
3 John's father's got his brother's coat. (possession/contraction: father has/possession)
4 When it's raining, that dog always stays in its kennel. (contraction)
5 It's easy to see how the cat shut its paw in the Browns' gate. (contraction/plural possession)
6 The hyenas' eyes were visible in the bushes everywhere we looked. (plural possession)

Chapter 4

Activity 1
1 Mrs Steele, letter, Queen
2 Bees, honey
3 Carlos, France, years

4 Mary, bike
5 Julius Caesar, Rome

Activity 2

Concrete	Abstract
1 water	life
2	exercise
	health
3 atmosphere	
bar	
smoke	
4 monk	understanding
5 members	
committee	strategy
6 Paul	philosophy

Activity 3

1 beautifully   5 harder, harder
2 slowly, silently 6 high
3 quickly   7 dearly
4 fast   8 rashly

Chapter 5

Activity 1

A

1 Jack said, "My partner is expecting a baby."
2 "I was born in Tunis," said Pierre.
3 "Where is the post office?" asked the tourist.
4 The toddler yelled, "I want an ice cream!"
5 "That dog," said John, "always disappears when I want to bath it."
6 "Why," asked Tom, "have you put the beer under my bed?"
   (Notice here that the question mark does not come after the word
   Why because that is not the end of the question.)

B

1 Mary said, "The eggs are in the fridge."
2 "High tide will be at three this afternoon," said the sailor.
3 "Come back here!" yelled the policeman.
4 Sam asked politely, "How much extra will I have to pay?"

5 "I haven't laughed so much," said Ben, "since the chicken coop collapsed."
6 "The main difficulty," explained the leader, "will be getting the tents across the river."

Activity 2
PART A
Disaster experts now hope that the Orissa cyclone will encourage the authorities to take similar safety measures.

"It is only when you have a serious cyclone and people see bodies lying around that people get stirred into action," says Geoffrey Dennis who heads the Red Cross in New Delhi.

PART B
Both scrambled out unhurt as the vehicle careered downhill, and could only watch in horror as it headed towards the converted former Methodist chapel owned by the Hawkins, who are potters.

"The possibilities were horrendous," said Mr Sloman, in shock after what he said had been a terrifying experience. "It was extremely wet and the vehicle aquaplaned on the grass, lost traction, and took off."

Witnesses said the Land-Rover bounced down the hillside like a tennis ball before plummeting through the slate roof of the pottery.

Activity 3
2 Mark said that he was driving a Ford then.
3 Mark said that he had driven to Italy the previous month.
4 Mark said that he had driven 500 miles that week.
5 Mark said that he had been driving for 10 years then.
6 Mark said that he had been driving at night when the brakes failed.
7 Mark said that he would drive to Spain the following year.
8 Mark said that he would be driving a Porsche the following year.
Note that in No. 6, it is not necessary to change the tense of 'failed'. The sense is clear.

Chapter 8

Activity 1
1 <u>There are fairies at the bottom of my garden</u> where I haven't cut the grass.
2 Although it's freezing, <u>I refuse to wear woolly undies</u>.

3 <u>Place all gallstones in the bucket provided</u> after you have sewn up the patient.

4 Coming out of the supermarket, <u>I bumped into a small horse</u>.

5 <u>A problem shared is a problem halved</u>, as long as the trouble is either legal or is not divulged to a serving police officer.

6 <u>It's hot</u>.

Chapter 9

Activity 2

<u>Register</u>	<u>Tone</u>
(a) estate agent's marketing language	positive, upbeat
(b) legal language	calm, serious
(c) technical writing (from instructions on fitting a shower)	unemotional

Index